WARNING:

This guide contains differing opinions. Hundreds of Heads will not always agree. Advice taken in combination may cause unwanted side effects. Use your head when selecting advice.

How to Get A's in College

in

Hundreds of Student-Tested Tips

FRANCES NORTHCUTT, SPECIAL EDITOR

Hundreds of Heads Books, LLC

ATLANTA

Cover photograph by JupiterImages
Cover and book design by Elizabeth Johnsboen

Library of Congress Cataloging-in-Publication Data

Northcutt, Frances.
  How to get A's in college : hundreds of student-tested tips / Frances Northcutt, special editor.
    p. cm.
  Includes bibliographical references.
  ISBN 978-1-933512-08-2
  1. Study skills—United States. 2. College student orientation—United States. 3. Test-
taking skills—United States. I. Title.
  LB2395.N67 2007
  378.1'70281--dc22
                    2007006278

See page 291 for credits and permissions.

HUNDREDS OF HEADS® books are available at special discounts when purchased in bulk for
premiums or institutional or educational use. Excerpts and custom editions can be created
for specific uses. For more information, please email sales@hundredsofheads.com or write
to:

HUNDREDS OF HEADS BOOKS, LLC
#230
2221 Peachtree Road, Suite D
Atlanta, Georgia 30309

ISBN-10: 1-933512-08-3
ISBN-13: 978-193351208-2

Printed in U.S.A.
10 9 8 7 6 5 4 3 2

CONTENTS

I got A's in college. I also got some B's. And two C-pluses—those still hurt! I had this idea that if I said what I thought in class, and wrote what I thought in my papers, I would earn grades exactly in line with my intelligence, and that would be the best I could do. It wasn't until I graduated and became an academic advisor for college students that I realized how wrong I had been.

At UC Berkeley my advisees inspired me through their efforts to grow as learners. Students became better writers not because they had a flash of inspiration while walking on the beach, but because they returned again and again to the college writing center. Some students who had breezed through high school ended up on probation after their first semester—and then made a triumphant recovery after they returned to basics, learning how to study and manage their time. I saw that students could change their academic performance, sometimes dramatically. Clearly, it was not all about being smart. So, what *was* it all about?

My students here in New York City don't just want to get A's—they *must* get A's or they will lose their scholarships. You may be in a similar program, or you may be in a place where "C's earn degrees", but you wish to do better. Regardless of the type of academic program you belong to, you have many demands on your time. Should you take the time to read this book? And should you take the even more time-consuming step of following the advice you will find here?

I know that you will save yourself both time and stress by informing yourself about strategies for college success. You can learn a lot from the students interviewed in this book. I also know that the techniques I recommend are worth a try. I have seen them work for hundreds of students—and one of those students is me.

Come to this book just as you would to an academic text: with an open, engaged, and curious mind. Adapt these ideas to fit your own life. Be willing to try new study methods and approaches, even if they don't come naturally at first.

I wish you academic success, this semester and always.

—FRANCES NORTHCUTT

THE HEADS EXPLAINED

With hundreds of tips, stories, and advice in this book, how can you quickly find those golden nuggets of wisdom? Of course, we recommend reading the entire book, but you can also look for these special symbols:

 Remember this significant story or advice.

 This may be something to explore in more detail.

 Watch out! Be careful! (Can we make it any clearer?)

 We are astounded, thrilled, or delighted by this one.

 Here's something to think about.

—*THE EDITOR*
AND HUNDREDS OF HEADS BOOKS

The Difference: You're Not in High School Anymore

In my last job, I taught a class called Developing Academic Success. Most of the students were there because they had had a particularly bad semester—they were on academic probation, had failed a course or two, or were in danger of not meeting the GPA requirements for their major. They joined the class (or were gently shoved into it by their advisors) in order to brighten up their attitude towards college and learn some useful study skills.

As you can imagine, the mood on the first day of class was not always very positive. It can be embarrassing to sit in a class and *have your classmates know that you are not happy with how you're doing in college. Usually, students like to keep this sort of thing to themselves. I would often break the ice in these class sessions by asking the students to guess what grade I got on my first college exam. The course was in Environmental Geology. I will tell you what I got: a 56 out of 100 points. That's an F by any standard; truly a terrible score.*

How did this happen? I was an honor student in high school; I won all kinds of academic prizes. I write this not to boast, but to illustrate how different academic expectations are in college compared to high school. In high school, I did very well without developing the best study habits. When I got that test paper back with the 56 on the last page, I realized that something had to change.

The students in my class always loved hearing about my big failure. There is a German word for taking joy in others' suffering: schadenfreude. It is a natural human emotion. But apart from schadenfreude, the students found my story encouraging because it confirmed the near universality of this experience: getting to college and finding that the old ways just don't yield the same results anymore.

The key to success in college academics is being ready to adapt to the new expectations. This chapter will give you some ideas on how to get started.

THE HARDEST TRANSITION from high school to college is learning to manage your time. Before college, your parents were constantly on you to keep up with your schoolwork. In college, you will only be spending a fraction of your time in class, compared to what you are used to. Studying right after my classes are done is the best option. That leaves the night open to hang out with friends and do all kinds of other things.

—KERRY COOLEY
LONG LAKE, MINNESOTA
🏛 VILLANOVA UNIVERSITY

In college, the professors come to lecture, say what they want to say, and then I'm on my own.

—CAO HONG
WALNUT,
CALIFORNIA
🏛 UNIVERSITY
OF CALIFORNIA,
LOS ANGELES
GPA: 3.95

WHERE I WENT TO COLLEGE at Ball State University, there are large lecture halls for some of the introductory classes. Being in a class with 60 or more students means it's easier to fall through the cracks and get lost; it forces you to take responsibility for coming to class, participating, and taking notes.

—GERRY APPEL
FORT WAYNE, INDIANA
🏛 BALL STATE UNIVERSITY

I USED TO HAVE TWO HOURS to complete an exam, and at UCLA I only have 50 minutes. It's hard for me because I usually need time to warm up when I take tests, but I just have to study harder and be more prepared.

—KRISTIN
INGLEWOOD, CALIFORNIA
🏛 UNIVERSITY OF CALIFORNIA, LOS ANGELES

COLLEGE WAS A SHOCK FOR ME. I came from small-town America. I lived outside Philadelphia with a bunch of cows. The biggest thing that happened to my town was Wal-Mart. Then I came to Boston University: Everybody and everything moved very fast. I learned that you have to watch how much you party, and you can't drink on a weeknight; you don't want to be hungover for class.

—RIDA
REDERACH, PENNSYLVANIA
BOSTON UNIVERSITY

• • • • • • • •

I thought I was the cream of the crop in high school, but when I got to my first college class I realized how average I was.

—JANET
LOS ANGELES, CALIFORNIA
UNIVERSITY OF CALIFORNIA, LOS ANGELES

• • • • • • • •

IN HIGH SCHOOL I WAS GIVEN my schedule on the first day of class; I didn't get to choose anything. Then I came to Berkeley, I got to choose my classes, which was so much more enjoyable.

—BRIAN
BABYLON, NEW YORK
UNIVERSITY OF CALIFORNIA, BERKELEY

FRAN'S FABLES: THE ANTS AND THE SEEDS

Two young ants needed to carry 120 seeds each over a perilous bridge above a roaring river. The wise old ant sunning himself on the riverbank told them to make eight trips, carrying 15 seeds at a time. But the young ants were impatient—they wanted to finish the job and start having fun. They put their tiny heads together and decided to carry 20 seeds at a time: then they would need to make only six trips. The ants loaded themselves up with 20 seeds each and started across the bridge.

They had gone only halfway across when their knees began to creak; soon two little ants and 40 seeds were bobbing downstream in the roaring river. The ants washed up on a sand bar and watched their seeds float away.

When the sun had dried them, they decided to try again. They marched back to where their remaining seeds waited. Fifteen seeds at a time, the ants carried their burden across the bridge. Then they went into the meadow to gather 40 seeds to replace those they had lost. Instead of rushing to finish the job, they explored every corner of the meadow and picked out the nicest seeds. When they approached the bridge again, they found that they had become strong enough to carry 20 seeds each across in one trip. And they did.

The moral of the story: Follow advice.

WHAT DO YOU EXPECT TO GET OUT OF COLLEGE?

MY EXPECTATIONS WERE TOO LOW. The only thing I expected out of college was a degree, and that's all I got.

> —ZAKIA SIPP
> CHICAGO, ILLINOIS
> CHICAGO STATE UNIVERSITY

• • • • • • • •

I EXPECTED TO WORK HARD in college and to study all the time. I imagined nothing but class, class, class, but I was wrong. While keeping my grades up, I ended up having fun doing things I didn't even know existed, such as fencing. I joined the fencing club and now I can duel with the best of them.

> —JANET
> LOS ANGELES, CALIFORNIA
> UNIVERSITY OF CALIFORNIA, LOS ANGELES

• • • • • • • •

I EXPECTED TO SPEND MY TIME in high-level intellectual engagement, day and night. That wasn't what I got, to say the least.

> —M.K.
> BROOKLYN PARK, MINNESOTA
> BELOIT COLLEGE GPA: 3.5

IN HIGH SCHOOL you don't have many choices; your class schedule is basically engraved in stone. In college you can drop classes up to two weeks into the term. When I took trigonometry in college, I hated it and I hated the professor. Two weeks into it I dropped it. I'm glad that I did because I took the class two years later with a different professor and did really well the second time around. I think the flexibility that comes with being in college can be used to your advantage.

— ANONYMOUS
LOS ANGELES, CALIFORNIA
UNIVERSITY OF CALIFORNIA, LOS ANGELES

• • • • • • • • •

IN A COLLEGE MATH CLASS, the lesson is often assigned before the professor goes over it. The professor wants students to try to learn it on their own first. Homework is often optional. The next day the professor will teach the lesson and answer any questions from students who did the homework; but overall he is not concerned whether each student in the class understands the material. He expects you to come to his office for additional help or get help from a tutor or a friend.

— LAURA
TINLEY PARK, ILLINOIS
BRADLEY UNIVERSITY

THE MOST SHOCKING DIFFERENCE to me between high school and college was the level of competitiveness among students. In high school only a select group of people did well enough to get into a good school. But at my college, everyone does well, everyone is really smart, and the entire student body is really competitive. I study at least ten hours a week to make sure I get the grades to make myself stand out.

—MICHAEL POWELL
GLENDALE, CALIFORNIA
UNIVERSTIY OF CALIFORNIA, BERKELEY GPA: 3.63

> College isn't that different from high school.
>
> —EVETTE WILLIS
> CHICAGO, ILLINOIS
> CHICAGO STATE UNIVERSITY

• • • • • • • •

IN MY COUNTRY, high school was from 8 a.m. until 4 p.m., and that did not include extracurricular activities. If you wanted to play sports or join a club, it had to start after school. My teachers and parents were strict, so slacking off wasn't an option. When I got to college and saw that all I had to do was read some chapters in a book to pass a test, I knew college would be a breeze.

—WANJIKU
CARBONDALE, ILLINOIS
ILLINOIS UNIVERSITY, CARBONDALE

• • • • • • • •

THERE WAS DEFINITELY a lot more reading than in high school. Also, there was not as much handholding. You have to do a lot outside of class. In high school you can get away with doing very little after school. Not in college.

—MOIRA
NEW YORK, NEW YORK
BOSTON COLLEGE

DON'T GIVE UP—ADAPT!

Some of the coolest and most successful students I have known started off with a bad semester, or had one along the way. What made them special was the way they picked themselves up, dusted themselves off, and went after their goal of academic improvement with humor, creativity, and determination.

One student stands out in this regard. Sheila enrolled in my college skills course when she was on probation and in danger of being dropped from her program. I noticed her right away because she sat in the front row, took notes during my lectures, and participated cheerfully in all the class activities. During the semester I found out that Sheila had a painful and chronic physical condition. Because her condition limited how much she could do each day, Sheila became an expert at maximizing her productive hours. She became incredibly organized, responsible, and proactive—and it began paying off. Before long, Sheila was earning A's and B's in all of her courses, and serving as a role model to other students.

As a former English major, I know that stories are very boring if the main character does not face some obstacles. You will probably face some obstacles during your college career; some of them may be big ones. Just try to remember that challenges are par for the course, and that every difficulty gives you the opportunity to be a hero, like Sheila.

DURING THE FIRST DAYS OF CLASSES every professor took attendance. I was freaked out, thinking that it was going to be just like high school, but I quickly realized that it was only a first-day thing. After the semester got into full swing, a lot of classes didn't check attendance. By December you can see why taking attendance isn't necessary; it's reflected in your grades.

—BRIDGET SCRABECK
LAKEVILLE, MINNESOTA
UNIVERSITY OF ST. THOMAS

The biggest difference: You really need to find a balance between partying and work.

—PAIGE HILL
MONTEREY, CALIFORNIA
UNIVERSITY OF CALIFORNIA, LOS ANGELES

I NEVER HAD TO STUDY IN HIGH SCHOOL. When I got to college, I thought I could still get away with not studying. So I just went to my lectures and took notes. I never opened up my books. As a result, I failed at least five tests before I humbled myself and opened a book.

—CORAVIECE TERRY
MOUNDS, ILLINOIS
SOUTHERN ILLINOIS UNIVERSITY, CARBONDALE

ACADEMICALLY, HIGH SCHOOL AND COLLEGE are about the same. You still have multiple-choice tests, essays, and working in groups. But socially, college was much easier. On a big campus, you don't have peer pressure to party, have sex, or watch TV all day. The pressure comes from within, and I learned that I can handle myself pretty well.

—A.P.
CHICAGO, ILLINOIS
MALCOLM X COLLEGE

YOU CAN'T DO NEARLY as many extracurricular activities as you did in high school. I signed up for a bunch of them when I got to college, but I had to quit the newspaper; I'd been very involved in that in high school.

—ANNA
PRINCETON, NEW JERSEY
PRINCETON UNIVERSITY

WHEN I CUT CLASSES IN HIGH SCHOOL, my homeroom teacher would deal with me and so would my parents; but in college there is no accountability. I didn't have to go to class, and nobody was going to call my mother. But at the end of semester, that 2.2 GPA was my accountability. I smelled the coffee after that.

—TODD LUCAS
CHICAGO, ILLINOIS
SOUTHERN ILLINOIS UNIVERSITY

GETTING MY FIRST-QUARTER GRADES was definitely a heart attack. I had very good grades in high school, but they weren't so great in college. After that, I took one less class to get my confidence up, talked to more people before registering to see if the teachers were difficult, asked around if there was someone who had taken the class and could help me. And I just studied; I went to the library and made myself stay there.

—CANDACE WATSON
LOS GATOS, CALIFORNIA
SANTA CLARA UNIVERSITY

IN HIGH SCHOOL I WAS ONE OF 10 valedictorians. I found it really easy to get A's in high school. I thought college would be no different. My first semester, I got the first B of my life. This was a turning point for me because I defined myself by my grades; just as one person might be good at sports, I was the one who had all of the answers. I suddenly realized I was surrounded by valedictorians and a lot of them were smarter than I was. Getting the B made me realize that life wasn't just about grades. I immediately decided I would become more social and focus instead on not getting C's.

—ROBERT
SCOTTS VALLEY, NEW JERSEY
UNIVERSITY OF CALIFORNIA, BERKELEY

• • • • • • • •

WE HAD 1,500 STUDENTS in my high school, and no more than 28 students in a class. Then I went to the University of Michigan. Intro to Chemistry had 500 students in it—basically my entire high school grade in this auditorium. But it didn't freak me out, because it was the same school-work. As long as you can hear your lecturer and see what's on the slides, you'll be okay.

—NICK
NEW CITY, NEW YORK
UNIVERSITY OF MICHIGAN

CHAPTER 2

Course Smarts: Choosing & Registering for Classes

The line starts at the door of your advisor's office, winds through the advising suite, and ends somewhere waaaay down the hall. It's no secret that the days leading up to registration are one of the busiest times for advisors. To get the most out of advising for course selection, be aware of deadlines and go to see your advisor well in advance. Even before the course schedule comes out, you can come up with some general ideas for what you would like to take and discuss them with your advisor. This is a great opportunity to impress *your advisor by being prepared and taking responsibility for coming up with a rough draft of a plan.*

You can stand out from the crowd by asking a few great questions. Want to become a better writer? Ask your advisor to recommend a writing intensive class. Feel a little bit unprepared in the hard sciences? Ask your advisor if he or she knows of a professor who has a reputation for being able to explain scientific concepts clearly. Need to explore a couple of different possible majors? Pick out a few introductory courses in those areas, and ask your advisor which he or she thinks are the best for you.

And when the next semester is well underway, be sure to stop by and let your advisor know how the classes you worked together to select are going!

I MADE SURE THAT I had a class every day of the week. That way, I wouldn't be tempted to stay in my dorm room all day and watch television. By having classes every day, I knew I had to get up, prepare myself, and get out of my room.

— TSHINO KANKWENDA
MONTREAL, CANADA
SOUTHERN ILLINOIS UNIVERSITY

• • • • • • • •

DON'T SCHEDULE CLASSES earlier than 10 a.m., especially on Fridays; you will not be able to get up. Often, students are drinking the night before or simply talking with friends until 3 a.m.

— ANONYMOUS
ST. LOUIS, MISSOURI
WASHINGTON UNIVERSITY IN ST. LOUIS

• • • • • • • •

I'M A MORNING PERSON, so I don't mind having an early class, but I've learned that I would rather schedule my classes for later in the day so I can take care of other things in the morning. I schedule my first class at noon so my mornings are free. I also try to have one day a week without any classes.

— MANPREET
LOS ANGELES, CALIFORNIA
UNIVERSITY OF SOUTHERN CALIFORNIA GPA: 3.9

TAKE COURSES JUST BECAUSE YOU WANT TO. Open your mind to things that may not relate to anything in the future. Don't fall for the tyranny of "career thinking" and take courses just because they may further a career. I took a painting course while majoring in economics. It used my brain in a different way and added a really fun and interesting dimension to my studies. I also met great people whom I would have never met otherwise.

—JANE
MONTCLAIR, NEW JERSEY
BARNARD COLLEGE

* * * * * * * *

I try to schedule my classes straight through the day, with no gaps in between. If there are gaps it's easier to make excuses not to go. If you have an hour and a half off between classes, you might go back to your room and take a nap, and there goes that day.

—*Anonymous*
Canoga Park, California
University of California, Berkeley GPA: 3.67

ONLINE RATINGS

AT MY SCHOOL THERE IS A WEB SITE started and run by students called yourteachers.com. Students post their feelings about teachers and rank them. You can make sure the teacher fits your style before you take his or her class.

> —KERRY COOLEY
> LONG LAKE, MINNESOTA
> VILLANOVA UNIVERSITY

• • • • • • • •

THE BEST TOOL AVAILABLE AT UCLA for choosing classes is bruinwalk.com. You can read reviews of professors written by other students. It rates professors on things like difficulty and approachability. I found it to be very accurate.

> —ANONYMOUS
> MODESTO, CALIFORNIA
> UNIVERSITY OF CALIFORNIA, LOS ANGELES

• • • • • • • •

STUDENTS' REVIEWS ARE GREAT as background, but take them with a grain of salt. If you see a general trend that the professor's a hard grader or never available to students, it's probably true. Obviously, the student who thinks she got an unfair grade will complain about the professor's standards; and the guy who never does any reading will definitely complain about the workload.

> —BAYLEE SIMON
> DEMAREST, NEW JERSEY
> MEDILL SCHOOL OF JOURNALISM GPA: 3.87

UNLESS YOU'RE IN LOVE with a certain professor or you've sworn to avoid a certain lecturer, always choose the right hours for classes. Even if you've signed up for Intro to Fiction with Chuck Palahniuk, History of White-Collar Crime with Jeff Skilling, or Advanced Coaching Techniques with Steve Spurrier, rainy November mornings and chilly February afternoons will happen, as will conflicts with other activities. Don't delay graduation by a year because you had to take that cooking class with Rachael Ray.

—SAM WEAVER
MINNEAPOLIS, MINNESOTA
MARQUETTE UNIVERSITY

JUST BECAUSE A CLASS IS PASS/FAIL doesn't mean it's a blowoff. I took a class called Applications in Quantum Mechanics because it's graded as pass or fail. You don't have to do everything right; you just have to do enough to pass. It's just not as easy as I though it would be. We do these problem sets that are incredibly hard; I have no idea how to even start. I sit there pulling out my hair, saying to myself, "I need to pass this class," instead of what I usually say to myself when I'm studying for other classes: "I need to get an A in this class."

—LEYAN LO
BASKING RIDGE, NEW JERSEY
CALIFORNIA INSTITUTE OF TECHNOLOGY GPA: 3.7

CHOOSING THE RIGHT PROFESSOR is more important than the time or day of the class. When I am choosing a professor for one of my major classes, I look for someone who is enthusiastic and has a lot of knowledge, and when I am choosing professors for my general education requirements I look for the ones who will keep me awake and interested in the subject.

—NOEL
VANCOUVER, CANADA
 UNIVERSITY OF SOUTHERN CALIFORNIA GPA: 3.72

As I GOT USED TO COLLEGE and got to know professors, there were certain ones I'd take any class with at any time. I'm not a huge history person, but my professor, Dr. Barr, made everything interesting, and I would have taken anything that man taught, even Underwater Basket Weaving at 5:45 a.m. I took a poetry class on Thursday night when I swore to keep that block of time open for *Friends,* the only show I watched that semester. But my favorite professor only taught poetry on Thursday nights, and he was brilliant, so I left *Friends* to my crappy VCR. I never actually managed to tape it: I think I set the channel wrong and got the mating habits of bats or something. But a good professor is much more important.

Consider

—JACLYN YOUHANA
LIBERTY TOWNSHIP, OHIO

WHICH KIND OF PROFESSOR?

There are at least three different kinds of professors out there. Some are here to do their own research and in order to do that they have to teach some classes. Those professors are very knowledgeable but they just hammer out the information in class and the students are left on their own to read the text and seek out TAs. Then there are other professors who are there just to teach; they love their subjects and want to share them with their students. They present information in a way that is easily understood. And finally, there are professors that hate to see students nodding off in lecture class and will just kick them out.

Choose professors who are known to be interesting. You can find them through word of mouth and through Web sites, like ratemyprofessor.com. But the best way to go about it is to talk to upperclassmen.

—EDWARD WEAVERLING
BERKELEY, CALIFORNIA
UNIVERSITY OF CALIFORNIA, BERKELEY

NOW THAT I'M IN MY FINAL YEAR of college and I have
more freedom in my course schedule, I choose classes
based on the instructors who are teaching them. I enjoy
professors who encourage a lively discussion in class and
let students debate, even if they disagree with the professor. I once took a class on poverty and the students
began debating the issue of welfare and poor, large families in America. The discussion was getting heated, and,
rather than let it run its course for the remaining three
minutes of class, my professor stopped it in its tracks
because she was too uncomfortable talking openly
about it.

—ROB J. METZLER
BUFFALO, NEW YORK
STATE UNIVERSITY OF NEW YORK, BUFFALO

• • • • • • • •

*If you failed your first test and still
have time to withdraw from class, please
do it. I had a Greek mythology course,
and I failed it because I didn't know
withdrawing was an option.*

—MELISSA BERNARD
COUNTRY CLUB HILLS, ILLINOIS
COLUMBIA COLLEGE

I ALWAYS TRIED TO CHOOSE more difficult classes when I put together my schedule. There are classes that you know you will do well in with the least effort, but the harder classes prepared me for the work I'm doing in graduate school.

—M.E.
ATHENS, GREECE
NATIONAL TECHNICAL UNIVERSITY OF ATHENS

Professors are liked by students for different reasons; ask around.

—KERRY COOLEY
LONG LAKE,
MINNESOTA
VILLANOVA
UNIVERSITY

MAKE SURE YOUR ADVISOR is doing his job. My academic advisor was not helpful. Instead of suggesting classes that would benefit me, he asked me what I wanted to take. He just put the classes into the computer to make sure they weren't closed. I didn't even know if they were required. So before the next registration period, my friends in my major gave me advice on what classes to take.

—WANJIKU
CARBONDALE, ILLINOIS
ILLINOIS UNIVERSITY, CARBONDALE

IF YOU HAVE TO FULFILL a general education course, or if you need extra credit hours, consider taking some sort of diversity class. I learned a lot about other cultures by doing this. College is about expanding your mind and learning new things, so why not learn more about the people around you?

—MANDY TAKACS
MEDINA, OHIO
BOWLING GREEN STATE UNIVERSITY

SENSING A PATTERN HERE ...

FRESHMAN YEAR, you sign up for Monday-Friday, 8 a.m. classes because you want to prove to yourself you're a go-getter and you can handle it.

SOPHOMORE YEAR, it's class at 10 a.m. every day.

JUNIOR YEAR, it's class at 12:30 p.m. on Monday, Wednesday, Friday, and you feel the upperclass slack coming on.

SENIOR YEAR, you only have class two or three days a week and it's still a struggle to get up because you're trying to enjoy sleeping in before you graduate and life's over.

—TOM M. NEMO
OAKDALE, MINNESOTA
UNIVERSITY OF MINNESOTA

I SHOULD BE CHOOSING CLASSES that will help me fulfill my major requirements, but instead I usually choose classes that just seem interesting to me. I would rather take classes about something I really want to learn and maybe stay here for an extra year. I don't want to put too much pressure on myself to graduate in four years. The way I look at it is I pay so much money to get my degree, so I am going to choose what I want to study and I am going to make the most of what my school has to offer. I will not get this opportunity again!

—SONIA MENDOZA
LOS ANGELES, CALIFORNIA
UNIVERSITY OF CALIFORNIA, LOS ANGELES

• • • • • • • •

You can't have early-morning classes after a night of partying. I had a class that I had to leave three times to vomit. Don't ever schedule morning classes after party night.

—LAUREN CRUZ
NEW YORK, NEW YORK
WESLEYAN UNIVERSITY

IF YOU REALLY WANT TO MAKE SURE you get a good professor, over-register for classes and sit in one or two lectures, look at the syllabus and then make your decision. One professor at my college won a Pulitzer Prize, and every history major says he's the greatest professor of all time. I found his lectures to be big snoozers. For another history class I had a teacher no one ever heard of and she was really good.

—ANONYMOUS
CANOGA PARK, CALIFORNIA
UNIVERSITY OF CALIFORNIA, BERKELEY GPA: 3.67

I ATTENDED A SMALL, LIBERAL ARTS SCHOOL because I wanted to take a diverse range of courses. I took advantage of the opportunity to learn things that I otherwise would not learn in my career track. For example, I took classes such as Introduction to Massage Therapy, Bowling, World Religions, and Culture of Brazil; they all broadened my experience and introduced me to students outside of my major.

—LEIGH
CHICAGO, ILLINOIS
WESLEYAN UNIVERSITY

FIVE TERRIBLE REASONS TO TAKE A CLASS

1. It meets in the afternoon, so you don't have to drag yourself out of bed too early in the day.
2. All your friends are taking it—you can hang out together in the back of the lecture hall and have fun!
3. Your grade is based on one paper that isn't due until the end of the semester. No problem; you can goof off all semester, then pull a few all-nighters at the end. A whole semester's worth of credit for just a few days of work—what a deal!
4. You looked up the professor on that Rate My Professors Web site and he or she has a reputation of being a really easy grader. What else could you ask for?
5. The classroom is in the building right next to where you live.

USE THE ADD/DROP PERIOD to dissect your syllabus. Read through the entire thing to see what kind of assignments and how many papers you'll have, how many exams you will have, and when they are given. Check for conflicts: You don't want to find yourself in the middle of the semester with four 15-page papers due in the same week, or with two cumulative exams scheduled on the same day. I learned this my sophomore year when I had two exams on the same day within an hour of each other. I ended up getting C's.

—YINKA
CLINTON, MARYLAND
UNIVERSITY OF PENNSYLVANIA

• • • • • • • •

NEVER CHOOSE A CLASS based only on the subject. It took me two years of college to learn not to take a course just because it sounds interesting. Talk to other students about the professor. If you are looking to go to graduate school where you will need a high GPA to get in, and the teacher for that class is tough, you can ruin your GPA. I took a Latin class on a poet that I really liked. Other students did not give the professor great reviews, but I tried it anyway. I ended up getting a low grade.

—JACK LIGMAN
LANCASTER, CALIFORNIA
UNIVERSITY OF CALIFORNIA, LOS ANGELES

There is nothing that can make a class good or bad as much as the professor.

—EUGENE
FOSTER CITY,
CALIFORNIA
UNIVERSITY
OF CALIFORNIA,
BERKELEY

I CHOSE A SCHEDULE where I would only have class once a week for three hours. I thought it would be perfect: I would have a whole week to complete my assignments. But I always waited until the day of the class to complete my work, and I didn't do well that semester. So I went back to having one-hour courses every other day; that kept me on my toes.

—CEDRIC MALONE
CARBONDALE, ILLINOIS
SOUTHERN ILLINOIS UNIVERSITY

• • • • • • • •

Do the research yourself by sitting in on classes early in the semester.

—ANONYMOUS
CANOGA PARK, CALIFORNIA
UNIVERSITY OF CALIFORNIA, BERKELEY GPA: 3.67

IF YOU ARE GOING TO COLLEGE to get good grades it's really important to feel out the appropriate classes for your major and which professors work for you. You should also try to find out about the workload; different professors for the same class may have different reading, paper and exam requirements.

—EDWARD WEAVERLING
BERKELEY, CALIFORNIA
UNIVERSITY OF CALIFORNIA, BERKELEY

• • • • • • • •

THE FIRST THING YOU SHOULD DO is to visit a counselor to get a general idea of what you want from college and how to achieve it. Then try to get information from other students about specific instructors.

—RUTH
BUENOS AIRES, ARGENTINA
CALIFORNIA STATE UNIVERSITY, NORTHRIDGE

TOO MANY COOL COURSES TO CHOOSE FROM?

This is a great problem to have, but it's a problem nonetheless. There's always a danger that you will graduate from college and realize that you took fascinating classes in a wide variety of areas, learned many interesting things, but never quite managed to put your selections together to make a coherent program: that's like going to a wonderful restaurant and ordering all the appetizers or all the desserts. The goal is to have a balanced academic program, just as we all strive for a balanced diet.

Try to look at the big picture, and map out a possible plan for all your remaining semesters, not just the next one. Are there some gaps in your general knowledge that you would like to fill in? Consider some broad survey courses as well as specialized ones. Review your college's general education requirements, and prepare a strategy for satisfying them with solid courses.

You don't have to do this alone! Your academic advisor can be a big help, of course. So can your professors. Ask your family for suggestions as well. They may have just the outside perspective that you need. And finally, if you adore a particular professor, take as many courses with him or her as you can. You will probably get more out of the experience than if you had taken just one course.

JUST AS A GREAT PROFESSOR can make something boring seem exciting, a bad one can make your favorite topic seem like oral surgery. I took 8 a.m. classes that at times seemed way too early, but were excellent because the classes were very small and the professors were dedicated. You will be much more likely to want to go to good early classes than bad late ones.

—EUGENE
FOSTER CITY, CALIFORNIA
UNIVERSITY OF CALIFORNIA, BERKELEY

• • • • • • • • •

ON A SCALE OF 1-10, I give my academic advisors a 6. They were like an automated telephone system that just told me the facts. I was expecting a person who loved the field and would be enthusiastic about giving me information beyond the mere required courses. They didn't motivate me at all, and when classes got tough, that's what I needed. Everybody needs a motivator to bring out the best in you.

—MARCHELLO HOLMAN
CHICAGO, ILLINOIS
SOUTHERN ILLINOIS UNIVERSITY

The Printed Word: Buying Books & the College Bookstore

I remember going to the bookstore at the beginning of my first semester of college, gathering an extremely tall, heavy stack of textbooks, and waiting for about 45 minutes in the long line at the cash register. Finally, I handed over my brand-new ID card to the clerk to complete the purchase. He handed it back, saying, "You can't do anything with this until you get your validation sticker."

I had to go back to campus (up a steep hill), get my sticker, then come back and start all over again. I almost cried.

I'm sharing this poignant tale of freshman cluelessness to make a point about how the actual purchase of books takes place only after you have completed many other steps. In my case, the missing step was obvious. But be careful not to miss another, less obvious step. In this chapter, students suggest many different ways to buy books—or get away with not buying them. But you should consider your individual needs as a student. For example, ordering books online might work well for you if your schedule is set far in advance, but not so well if you'll need to make many changes at the start of the semester. Buying older editions of textbooks might be a problem if you are studying a rapidly evolving field, but work out fine if you're not; you get the picture.

And a word of advice, for those times when you are so short on cash that you literally have no money for books when the semester begins: don't suffer in silence. Many colleges have an emergency loan fund for situations like this. You may be able to borrow a few hundred dollars and pay it back later in the year, interest-free. Ask your academic advisor—you won't be the first or the last.

I ALWAYS CHOSE THE USED TEXTBOOKS that were least highlighted. You never know if the last person was actually smart or just an over-highlighter.

—JULIA JAWORSKI
BLOOMFIELD HILLS, MICHIGAN
MICHIGAN STATE UNIVERSITY GPA: 3.83

• • • • • • • •

I DON'T BUY ANY OF MY BOOKS until after the first week of class starts, to avoid lines and chaos. When I first got here, I'd wait in line for about an hour—it would wrap around every single bookshelf—then we'd get to class and the teacher would say you need this, or you don't need this. Who does homework in the first week of school anyway? Figure out what books you need after the first week of school, and then go get them.

—A.K.
POUND RIDGE, NEW YORK
BOSTON COLLEGE

• • • • • • • •

I HATED BUYING BOOKS that I knew I wouldn't really need so I'd try to get any books I couldn't find online at the library. Some of my summer classes were really short, and taking books from the library worked. I would just get the book, read for an hour, take notes, and leave. Some of my friends would get their books from the library and photocopy them.

—LINDA SIN
PASADENA, CALIFORNIA
UNIVERSITY OF CALIFORNIA, BERKELEY

IF YOU GO TO THE BOOKSTORE and there's no list of books for your class, ask a manager or someone who has worked there awhile. They might say, "He never tells us ahead of time, but he always ends up using this book anyway." Or, "He always just uses excerpts from books you can get in any library." That helps a lot, and it is better to go ahead and buy something they recommend. If you wait, you might have to buy a new copy; the used ones always go first.

—J.B.
JACKSON, MICHIGAN
UNIVERSITY OF MICHIGAN GPA: 3.5

. . . .

I would check out the assigned book at the library: the professors would put them on reserve. Sometimes I'd make copies of only the important pages for eight cents a copy.

—NORRIS THOMPSON
CHICAGO HEIGHTS, ILLINOIS
SOUTHERN ILLINOIS UNIVERSITY

SOME PROFESSORS RARELY, if ever, use the assigned text-books. I've taken several classes with professors who told us that the textbooks weren't required reading or were simply for students' reference. Since you can find any type of information on the Internet (and for free!) why waste the money when it can be better spent going out to dinner instead of eating in the dining hall.

—BAYLEE SIMON
DEMAREST, NEW JERSEY
🏛 MEDILL SCHOOL OF JOURNALISM GPA: 3.87

- - - - - - - - -

I ALWAYS LOOK FOR supplementary materials to help me through my classes. I'm always looking for outlines online and I try to find other books that other teachers use or maybe some that my teacher used to use. In a class I'm taking now, my TA said that the book on the syllabus was not going to help. He suggested I purchase a few other books not even on the list.

—ANONYMOUS
FLAGSTAFF, ARIZONA
🏛 UNIVERSITY OF ARIZONA

- - - - - - - - -

I JUST LOVE BUYING FRESH, NEW TEXTBOOKS at the start of the term. Then I mark them up with colored pens and highlighters, and after finals I sell them back to the bookstore.

—MARGE
PRAIRIE VILLAGE, KANSAS
🏛 ST. OLAF COLLEGE

You have to be aggres-sive. I wanted to make sure that the bookstore did not run out

—PAIGE HILL
MONTEREY,
CALIFORNIA
🏛 UNIVERSITY
OF CALIFORNIA,
LOS ANGELES

ONLINE TEXTBOOK SHOPPING

BUYING BOOKS ONLINE MAY BE CHEAPER, but you have to make absolute certain you order—and receive—the right edition of every book. Sometimes teachers will give you exact page numbers to read, and if you have a different edition of the book, you'll be in trouble.

—DAWN RICHEY
RIPLEY, OHIO
XAVIER UNIVERSITY

• • • • • • • •

FIND OUT THE ISBN NUMBERS of the required books and go to allbookstores.com. They'll send you price quotes from 20 online booksellers.

—ANONYMOUS
ST. LOUIS, MISSOURI
WASHINGTON UNIVERSITY IN ST. LOUIS GPA: 3.7

• • • • • • • •

THE FIRST COUPLE OF YEARS, I was suckered into paying the bookstore prices. Then I wised up and bought and sold my books online. I'd estimate I've saved over $500 for four semesters worth of books this way. For the lazier times, selling back your books is a huge bonus.

—LAURA GLASS
GOLDEN VALLEY, MINNESOTA
MINNESOTA UNIVERSITY OF ST. THOMAS

DON'T BUY ALL THE BOOKS on the course syllabus—wait to see if you actually need them. Then, get them on amazon.com or half.com. If you do buy at the bookstore, and then find them online for a cheaper price, you can return the books to the bookstore for a full refund.

—S.S.
CURLEW, WASHINGTON
WASHINGTON UNIVERSITY IN ST. LOUIS

• • • • • • • •

MY FIRST SEMESTER HERE, I bought my books at the bookstore just because I didn't know any better. Now I buy them on amazon.com because they are cheaper. I pay two dollars for a book on Amazon, and at the bookstore they sell that same book for 10 dollars.

—MANPREET
LOS ANGELES, CALIFORNIA
UNIVERSITY OF SOUTHERN CALIFORNIA GPA: 3.9

• • • • • • • •

THE AVERAGE COST OF MY BOOKS at the bookstore was $500. I could buy the same books online for $200. I checked that I had the right edition by going to the bookstore and copying down the ISBN numbers off the books. I would then go to www.half.com, enter the ISBN, and find the book that I needed. It does take a few days for the books to arrive in the mail, so order them early.

—NATALEE
MARTINS FERRY, OHIO
XAVIER UNIVERSITY

I HAVE A FRIEND WHO SPENDS absolutely no money on books. He goes to the bookstore every day, finds the books he needs and hides somewhere in the shelves reading his assignment for the next class.

—MICHELLE WADDELL
HOLLYWOOD, FLORIDA
WASHINGTON UNIVERSITY IN ST. LOUIS GPA: 3.38

• • • • • • • •

> *You can buy cheat sheets for your classes from the bookstore. Ask for the "quick study guides."*
>
> —CESAR MEJIA
> LOS ANGELES, CALIFORNIA
> UNIVERSITY OF CALIFORNIA, BERKELEY GPA: 3.89

BUY YOUR BOOKS FROM student-run organizations. We have something called the Sophomore Honorary Lock and Chain that buys books from students and when they sell them, some of the profits go to charity. Your books are less expensive, and you're doing something good.

—C.K.
PEORIA, ILLINOIS
UNIVERSITY OF WASHINGTON

• • • • • • • •

THE BOOKS FOR MY CLASSES cost hundreds of dollars at the college bookstore. But I knew people who had taken the same class the year before and they usually just gave me the book because they didn't want it anymore. The bookstore would buy back used books for only a fraction of what they were worth. Sometimes the books were dog-eared or marked up, but I was happy to deal with some highlighted pages to save a few hundred bucks.

—ETHAN
MILFORD, CONNECTICUT
SOUTHERN CONNECTICUT STATE UNIVERSITY

I HAD A TEACHER WHO WROTE her own book and included it in the course reading list. She wanted every student to buy her book, which cost about $40, but there were a few copies at the school library, so I checked out the book and kept renewing it throughout the semester. I saved $50 and still got a B in the class.

—ETHAN
MILFORD, CONNECTICUT
SOUTHERN CONNECTICUT STATE UNIVERSITY

. . . .

IN ORDER TO AVOID CROWDS, I go first thing in the morning, or else I wait until the second week of class. I would not recommend the latter though, because although you may find yourself in front of the checkout line, you'll be behind everyone else in your class.

—ANONYMOUS
MODESTO, CALIFORNIA
UNIVERSITY OF CALIFORNIA, LOS ANGELES

. . . .

I LEARNED TO WAIT A *month* to buy my textbook, to see if I really needed it. My zoology professor had lectured from the whole book verbatim, and I did not have to open up that $88 book once. And when I tried to sell it back, the bookstore wouldn't take it because a new edition had been published.

—KARINNE SPENCER
CHICAGO, ILLINOIS
SOUTHERN ILLINOIS UNIVERSITY

FUN FACT

A century and a half ago, higher education was almost entirely closed to women. Sarah Grimké wrote:

"How many millions are invested in colleges, universities, Theological Seminaries for the education and exaltation of *men* to prepare them to fill offices of honor, trust and emolument? Is there one million invested for such purposes for the benefit of women? Nay, they not only are not blest with such patronage, but are even deprived of property by legal enactments, so that they can do very little for themselves."

Today, more than half of all college students in the United States of America are women. That's progress!

CHAPTER 4

Class Time: Lectures, Discussions & Taking Notes

I once read an interesting article that explored why so few movies and television shows focus on the academic side of college life. There are plenty that show college students falling in love, driving around, dealing with substance-abuse problems, fighting with their parents, and falling in love again. It's just that no one ever seems to go to class, meet up with a study group, or research a paper. Why is this? The article theorized that the nitty-gritty details of education just aren't filmic. You can't make a dramatic montage out of an organic chemistry lecture. There's no alternative to going through it minute by minute, just like in real life.

That's what's hard about classes: there's no shortcut, no condensed version, no sound bite that will substitute adequately for the real thing. Classroom learning is a slow, gradual process with only occasional moments of epiphany.

The saying, "it's a marathon, not a sprint" definitely applies here. You'll need to lace up your running shoes and get ready to put in a steady effort throughout the semester. Read on for some helpful coaching!

SHOWING UP IS HALF THE BATTLE. Once you miss a few classes, it's easy to fall behind, and it can be almost impossible to catch up.

> —LISA E. USCHAKOW
> LEVITTOWN, NEW YORK
> JOHN JAY COLLEGE OF CRIMINAL JUSTICE

• • • • • • • • •

LOTS OF STUDENTS THINK they can skip lectures: The professor won't know I'm there anyway, so what's the big deal? *Wrong!* You are paying money for these classes; just go! The best part of these classes are that when you go, you have to do less outside reading because you retain the same information from the lecture. The bad part: It is hard to focus because there are so many students in the class.

> —RICK HURCKES
> CHICAGO, ILLINOIS
> UNIVERSITY OF DENVER

• • • • • • • • •

ON THE FIRST DAY OF my freshman year there were about 150 students in my lecture hall. By midterms only 50 of them were showing up. Since almost all of our assignments are based on the textbook material, and one problem can take anywhere from four hours to a whole day to complete, why would anyone want to go sit in a one-hour lecture when they can be spending the time completing their assignments?

> —MARISSA CEVALLOS
> CHARLESTON, WEST VIRGINIA
> CALIFORNIA INSTITUTE OF TECHNOLOGY

CRUSH: STUDY AID OR CONCENTRATION KILLER?

THERE WAS THIS BOY IN MY HISTORY CLASS: he had to be the cutest boy ever. He never understood what was going on in class and he always asked me to explain it. I would study the lessons the night before so I could explain everything to him. That was the first time I really studied for a class. I got an A. Maybe I need a cute, dumb boy in all my classes!

—LESLEY
ORLAND PARK, ILLINOIS
BALL STATE UNIVERSITY

• • • • • • • • •

I ONCE HAD A CRUSH ON A GIRL in my class. One night a group of us were working on our problem sets, and one of the guys wrote something I can't repeat here, on my homework. It was about the girl and what we would do together. I forgot to erase it before I turned in my homework: when I got it back, the TA had written something like, "So how did it go?"

—S.P.
DHAKA, BANGLADESH
STANFORD UNIVERSITY

I HAD A CRUSH ON THE BOY who sat next to me during math class. We'd talk on occasion but because he didn't take notes at all, I felt like a loser writing down every word out of the calc professor's mouth. Bad idea. Luckily, he stopped coming to class. Then I took better notes and my grades improved.

—NICOLE SPENCE
ATLANTA, GEORGIA
EMORY UNIVERSITY GPA: 3.71

• • • • • • • •

HAVING A CRUSH ON A GIRL in class is inevitable but detrimental to your success. You end up thinking about her rather than about what the professor is saying. Get her attention by speaking up in class, saying stuff that is either very intelligent or very funny. But don't talk all the time; girls don't like brownnosers.

—ZACHARY URNESS
POLSON, MONTANA
UNIVERSITY OF ST. THOMAS

• • • • • • • •

IF YOU DO HAVE A CRUSH ON SOMEONE, put it aside when you're studying. One way to do that is to grab a midnight snack together *after* studying, or to make a plan to hang out *after* the test to celebrate together. You'll have something to look forward to.

—MICHAEL ABRAMOVITZ
ALTA LOMA, CALIFORNIA
UNIVERSITY OF ARIZONA GPA: 2.65

I HAD A CRUSH ON A GIRL ONCE; A friend of mine got her schedule so that I could sign up for some of the same classes. My attendance record in those classes was perfect, but I could not concentrate. I spent most classes doodling her name on my notebook.

—ANONYMOUS
EAST BRUNSWICK, NEW JERSEY
GEORGE WASHINGTON UNIVERSITY

• • • • • • • •

MY FAVORITE PROFESSOR IN COLLEGE was also my biggest crush. He was very handsome, had a full beard, wore wire-rimmed glasses and thick wool sweaters, and taught Romantic Poetry. I studied very hard and did well in the class for the obvious reason. You never want to disappoint the person you have the hots for.

—STEVE
SOUTH ORANGE, NEW JERSEY
UNIVERSITY OF CALIFORNIA, RIVERSIDE GPA: 3.5

• • • • • • • •

THERE WAS A GIRL IN MY FRESHMAN chemistry class whom I had the biggest crush on. Chemistry was probably my worst subject, but when I found out she needed help in the class I really pushed myself to learn it so I could offer to help her. I never got up the courage to approach her, but I did get an A in the class.

—J.A.
BOSTON, MASSACHUSETTS
UNIVERSITY OF SOUTHERN CALIFORNIA GPA: 3.8

LECTURE CLASSES ARE SO HUGE that no one even notices if you are there, but if you decide to skip, make sure you keep up with the reading. I blew off my classes but I made sure I read everything, and carefully. I took History of Rock and Roll: The professor was really good, but the class interfered with my work schedule so I missed it often. I listened to all of the CDs for the course, read the text, and ended up doing really well.

—J.R.
AUSTIN, TEXAS
UNIVERSITY OF TEXAS, AUSTIN

I sit closest to the aisle and closest to the door in lecture class. If there is an emergency I'm one of the first people out.

—J.T.
BURBANK, CALIFORNIA
UNIVERSITY OF CALIFORNIA, LOS ANGELES GPA: 3.3

MOST OF MY CLASSES had a large lecture a couple of times a week and smaller discussions once a week. Participate in the smaller discussions: It helps out the graduate student who is usually teaching the smaller discussion and it makes class time go faster.

—ADELAIDE WEAVER
WOODBURY, MINNESOTA
UNIVERSITY OF MINNESOTA

FUN NOTE-TAKING TIPS FOR VISUAL LEARNERS

If you're a visual learner, you can really have some fun with your class notes. Try these tips for creating notes that are mini works of art—and help you learn.

1. Use different colors of ink for different kinds of information. For example, if you're taking a philosophy class and learning about several great thinkers, assign each one a different color. You'll find that you remember the concepts much more easily, and you won't confuse the philosophers with one another. Studying languages? Try using one color for feminine words and another for masculine words.

2. Use different colors of paper for each class. You might choose green for biology, for example, and pink for that English class on romantic poetry. You can even color-match your folders and index cards. Soon, the instant you see green you'll start thinking about cell membranes.

3. Sometimes, as they say, a picture is worth a thousand words. Use concept maps and diagrams, as well as words, to record class lectures. Your college skills center can give you information on some mapping formats, and you can make up your own as well. It doesn't matter if no one else can read your concept maps, as long as they make sense to you.

YOU MIGHT THINK YOUR CLASS is boring and have trouble staying awake. But it might not be the subject that's putting you to sleep; it's probably where you are sitting. I once had perhaps the most interesting class ever—forensics—and even that was hard to pay attention to when I sat in the back.

—RICK HURCKES
CHICAGO, ILLINOIS
UNIVERSITY OF DENVER

• • • • • • • • •

MY BIOLOGY TEACHER caught me when I fell asleep in a 200-person class. I was very much asleep, almost to the point where drool was coming out of my mouth. People nudged me because she was calling my name. I dropped my books on the floor as I woke up. I remember her saying, "It's so nice of you to join us again."

—ROBERT
WINSTON-SALEM, NORTH CAROLINA
WESLEYAN UNIVERSITY

• • • • • • • • •

I LIKE LECTURE CLASSES because when you don't want to participate you can sit farther back. But when I want class to feel more personal I sit up close. When you're in the first three rows, almost everyone else is behind you and the professor is directly in front of you. You feel almost as if you're the only one there.

—ANONYMOUS
MODESTO, CALIFORNIA
UNIVERSITY OF CALIFORNIA, LOS ANGELES

> *I always try to sit in the front of the lecture hall. I used to sit in the back and fall asleep.*
>
> —CURTIS
> MISSION VIEJO,
> CALIFORNIA

TALKING (OR NOT) IN CLASS

PARTICIPATING IN CLASS DISCUSSIONS can either hurt you or help you. Doing it just to hear your own voice is going to annoy not only everyone else in the class, but the professor as well. But it is a way to get the teacher to discover who you are. If you are a student who will one day need letters of recommendation, it will open up more opportunities to talk to them.

—RACHEL ALDRICH
BROOKLYN PARK, MINNESOTA
UNIVERSITY OF WISCONSIN GPA: 3.7

• • • • • • • •

YOU CAN'T REPLACE THE CLASSROOM environment. There's lots of discussion, you have the chance to ask questions, and you're absorbing the information while you're taking notes. Some students think they can just borrow notes and read chapters in the book and they'll be up to date, but that's not what happens. One teacher gave us an open-notebook test, and some people still couldn't pass because they hadn't been there often enough.

—LISA E. USCHAKOW
LEVITTOWN, NEW YORK
JOHN JAY COLLEGE OF CRIMINAL JUSTICE

IF *YOU* DON'T PARTICIPATE IN CLASSROOM discussions, those budding law students who enjoy hearing themselves talk *will*. And if you ever find yourself in liberal arts classes, the aspiring attorneys of America will be sure to keep their voices up and your naptime down.

—SAM WEAVER
MINNEAPOLIS, MINNESOTA
MARQUETTE UNIVERSITY

• • • • • • • •

WHILE CLASSROOM DISCUSSION may seem less than appealing, it can make all the difference when your professor has to give you a "participation" grade. Even if you're not completely sure of yourself, professors love students who at least make an attempt.

—JENNIFER STOUT
BONFIELD, ILLINOIS
OLIVET NAZARENE UNIVERSITY

• • • • • • • •

I AM AN ACTIVE PARTICIPANT in class discussions; it helps me do better in the course. By voicing opinions or arguments you can bond with your classmates and your teacher while boosting your own participation grade. And, in those classes that require participation, I usually leave the class much more educated about my peers and much closer to my professors.

—BRIDGET SCRABECK
LAKEVILLE, MINNESOTA
UNIVERSITY OF ST. THOMAS

WHEN SHARING WITH THE CLASS, start off with something broad, like, "In relation to … " and then use a transitional phrase. In small classes it's all about transitional phrases. You'll be all set.

—GAVIN BODKIN
BRADFORD, NEW HAMPSHIRE
WESLEYAN UNIVERSITY

• • • • • • • •

IF YOU HAVE NO IDEA what you're talking about, I suggest keeping quiet. Some professors will jump all over you if you sound like an idiot. On the other hand, and I know this may sound shocking, you actually *learn* more when you participate in class discussions. It keeps you listening and thinking versus daydreaming about the hottie in the next row.

—JACLYN YOUHANA
LIBERTY TOWNSHIP, OHIO

• • • • • • • •

IF YOU WANT TO LOOK SMART and if you have a professor who posts the lectures online in advance, you can go over them way ahead, then ask the professor questions about what is coming up. Questions like, "How does this relate to (a future topic)?" Or, "What about (a future topic)?" It's a way to get your participation points.

—RYAN NAUGHTON
MAPLEWOOD, MINNESOTA
UNIVERSITY OF ST. THOMAS

CHALLENGE YOURSELF. I excelled in classes that expected—and sometimes demanded—more participation, primarily because that dynamic made me demand more of myself and prepare a bit more for each class. I also retained and processed the information better because there was a lot more active thinking involved. In classes where the professor just sat up there and talked, I could easily slip into "cruise-control" and coast for 45 minutes.

—C.F.
BROOKLYN, NEW YORK
DARTMOUTH COLLEGE GPA: 3.5

THE KEY TO DOING WELL in a lecture class is finding a seat where you can focus. My seat depended on the subject: For a history class, I would sit up front because history was boring and the teacher was literally three feet away from me. For classes that I didn't like, I would sit toward the back because I'm not good at hiding my facial expressions. When I liked a class I would sit in the middle.

—AUTUMN BYERS
LAFAYETTE, CALIFORNIA
UNIVERISTY OF CALIFORNIA, BERKELEY

* * * * * * * *

WHEN I WALKED INTO my first class at Sonoma State, I was overwhelmed by the size of the room and the number of students in the class. The front row was empty, and I ended up sitting there. The front row turned out to be the best place to sit in a lecture class. I sat there for the rest of the semester and chose that spot in other classes, as well.

—LIZ A. POPE
AUBURN, CALIFORNIA
SONOMA STATE UNIVERSITY

* * * * * * * *

SITTING IN FRONT in a big lecture hall helps you see the material and lets the teacher know you are paying attention.

—JODIE PIETRUCHA
MISHAWAKA, INDIANA
INDIANA UNIVERSITY, SOUTH BEND

HOW TO GET AN A WITHOUT GOING TO CLASS

This tactic generally only works in large lecture classes, but when you can pull it off, it makes you feel all warm and tingly—similar to finding $20 in the middle of a parking lot. The key is to sign up for a class with a professor who lectures straight from the textbook and ,tests from it, too. If you're disciplined enough to do reading on your own and study for exams from your notes, this type of class is a great way to boost your GPA from the comfort of your own bed.

During my sophomore year, I hit the jackpot by taking a philosophy class with a professor who might as well have been a walking, breathing textbook. During the whole quarter, I went to three classes—the first, the midterm and the final. And I got an A.

One key pointer to this is attending discussion sections led by TAs. These discussions tend to be smaller (only about 20-30 students) and meet once a week for an hour. In large classes, TAs have more influence over your grades than professors, so it behooves you to show your face to the grad student leading discussion, even if you flake out on class.

—Baylee Simon
Demarest, New Jersey
Medill School of Journalism GPA: 3.87

IT'S SO IMPORTANT TO GO TO CLASS. In my science classes I really didn't get as much from textbooks as I got from lectures. A lot of things they teach aren't even published yet. And If you don't take good lecture notes it's almost impossible to do well. If you miss one lecture you are completely lost.

—ANONYMOUS
IRVINE, CALIFORNIA
UNIVERSITY OF CALIFORNIA, SAN DIEGO

• • • • • • • •

> Try to limit yourself to two comments per class period; this way, the professor can get through the lecture and let you out early.
>
> —RYAN NAUGHTON
> MAPLEWOOD, MINNESOTA
> UNIVERSITY OF ST. THOMAS

DON'T THINK YOU CAN HIDE in a big lecture class. I had one of the most boring, monotonous philosophy professors ever. One time, I got up to sneak out of his class, and he put me on the spot in front of 200 students, yelling, "I see you're leaving: Goodbye, have a good day. Everyone say goodbye to your classmate who has somewhere better to be."

—TODD LUCAS
CHICAGO, ILLINOIS
SOUTHERN ILLINOIS UNIVERSITY

• • • • • • • •

I'M NOT REALLY A NOTE-TAKING TYPE of student, with the exception of one class. It was Abnormal Psychology, and was strictly a fast-paced lecture. My advice for classes like that: Write like hell!

—LEIGH
CHICAGO, ILLINOIS
WESLEYAN UNIVERSITY

IT WAS KIND OF SCARY the first time I walked into a lecture hall. I kept telling myself, "Don't trip and fall on your face in front of everyone." I avoided that scenario by sitting in the front of the room. Anyway, sitting up front is much better for learning and paying attention.

> —PAIGE HILL
> MONTEREY, CALIFORNIA
> UNIVERSITY OF CALIFORNIA, LOS ANGELES

* * * * * * * *

ALWAYS SIT IN THE FRONT ROW, to the left or right of the lecturer. I think sitting in front forces me to stay engaged, and awake! I sit to one side or the other so I can always view the board or screen on each side equally, otherwise, the instructor blocks it by being in the middle.

> —A.S.
> CHICAGO, ILLINOIS
> UNIVERSITY OF WISCONSIN

* * * * * * * *

IN CLASSES WHERE THERE IS ASSIGNED READING, the lecture typically summarizes everything that was important from the reading. There's usually so much reading that it's easy to fall behind. Just remember, anything assigned that isn't mentioned in lecture is more or less unimportant; if you can understand the lecture well, you can probably pull at least a B in the class.

> —EUGENE
> FOSTER CITY, CALIFORNIA
> UNIVERSITY OF CALIFORNIA, BERKELEY

TOP FIVE MISTAKES STUDENTS MAKE IN LARGE LECTURE CLASSES

1. **Not going to class:** The class is so huge that the professor doesn't know anyone's name. Is it really important to go to class if no one is taking attendance? The answer is yes, absolutely. Attending class and paying attention to the lecture is the most efficient way for you to learn the material.
2. **Sitting in the back:** Sure, it's comfortable back there and you can chat with your friends. But paying attention in a large lecture class is hard enough already. Do you really want to make it any harder?
3. **Not buying the textbook:** True, textbooks are incredibly expensive. It can be so easy to convince yourself that you won't really need the book as long as you pay attention in class and take good notes. Or you might try to save money by sharing a book with your friend. Unfortunately, these money-saving schemes will cost you in the long run. Buy the book, and make sure you put in the time and effort to get the most out of it. Your transcript will thank you!

4. **Enjoying the anonymity:** The class may be enormous, but you should still make it a goal to become acquainted with the professor. Say hello before or after class, or go to office hours. You will still be a face in the crowd, but you can become a familiar face.

5. **Eating in class:** Don't be the person disturbing every-one else with loud chewing noises, slurps, and the crackle of plastic takeout containers. You want your professor and classmates to think of you as "the one with the good ideas," not "the one with the nachos."

THREE WAYS TO STAY AWAKE IN CLASS

1. **Fuel up!** Remember your parents telling you that breakfast is the most important meal of the day? If you are taking a morning class, whether you eat breakfast or not can make or break your performance. Even if all you can manage is a granola bar, be sure to consume it before you walk through the lecture hall door.
2. **Sit up!** Up front, that is. It's much harder to fall asleep when the professor's eye is on you.
3. **Meet up!** Make a date with a friend in the same class to share notes later in the day. It's harder to slack off if you know you would be letting down a friend.

WHEN I'M BORED IN CLASS, I'll start doodling. I become focused on the doodling, and my notes end up making no sense. It's funny, the way English class can turn into an art class. Don't get too carried away with the creative aspect of the pen. When it comes to test time, all you'll have to rely on is that cool dragon that you drew.

—GAVIN BODKIN
   BRADFORD, NEW HAMPSHIRE
   WESLEYAN UNIVERSITY

I TAKE NOTES BY CATEGORIZING what the instructor is saying and immediately note what I feel are the main points in each category. When I start to study for an exam, I condense my notes and the important points.

—A.S.
CHICAGO, ILLINOIS
UNIVERSITY OF WISCONSIN

• • • • • • • • •

On the first day of class, exchange contact information with a couple of other students. That way, if you ever miss a class you can get the notes from them.

— MELISSA BARBAGALLO DAVIS
BALTIMORE, MARYLAND
UNIVERSITY OF MARYLAND

THREE WAYS TO MAKE A BAD FIRST IMPRESSION IN CLASS

1. Show up late on the first day of class.
2. Announce to your neighbors that you're only taking the class because it's a requirement.
3. Fall asleep.

WHEN I TAKE NOTES, I write down in my own words what the professor is saying. I had a tutor once who quizzed me on a lecture; I realized I understood nothing that I had written down in my notebook. My tutor said that the reason I didn't remember anything was because I was too worried about getting down every last word my professor was saying. Taking it all down verbatim is useless. You will not remember something unless you understand it first.

—SONIA MENDOZA
LOS ANGELES, CALIFORNIA
UNIVERSITY OF CALIFORNIA, LOS ANGELES

. . . .

I DO MORE LISTENING than note-taking. I want to give my full attention to what's being said so I can process it and truly understand the material. Although sometimes I worry that I won't remember everything, most of the time I do well when test time comes.

—ROB J. METZLER
BUFFALO, NEW YORK
STATE UNIVERSITY OF NEW YORK, BUFFALO

. . . .

I HAD PROFESSORS who put their notes on an overhead projector for us to copy down. But it's easy to mindlessly copy the words without absorbing any of the information. I would try to think about everything I was writing down, which made it stick in my head.

—AMANDA TUST
EAST STROUDSBURG, PENNSYLVANIA
UNIVERSITY OF SAN DIEGO

I PAY CAREFUL ATTENTION to what my professor empha-
sizes during class. When he or she says something loudly
or repeats information, I know I should get it down in my
notebook. If I do happen to miss something important, I
ask a classmate to fill me in after class or I write down a key
word and look it up later in the textbook. I also created
my own form of shorthand so I can take notes faster. In
my philosophy class last year, I shortened "Plato" to "Pl"
and "important" (a word I noticed instructors use often)
to "imp."

—JADE STANFIELD
WARNER ROBINS, GEORGIA
NORTHWESTERN UNIVERSITY

• • • • • • • •

I HAVE SUCH SLOPPY HANDWRITING that if I did take notes
I wouldn't be able to read them. If you can't take good
notes, you have to get other people to take them for
you, or purchase them from a note-taking company like
the one at my university. They hire someone from the
class to take notes for the entire semester, and then they
sell those notes online.

—ANONYMOUS
CANOGA PARK, CALIFORNIA
UNIVERSITY OF CALIFORNIA, BERKELEY GPA: 3.67

NOTE TAKING: QUALITY, NOT QUANTITY

When I ask students if they are happy with their note-taking skills, they often reply, "I'm great at taking notes! I write down every word the professor says!" I have to congratulate the students on their speed, and I am amazed by their three-ring binders full of closely written pages. Unfortunately, this is not the right way to go.

Note taking serves two purposes. First, there's the *process.* As you listen to the lecture and look at the visual aids, you process the information and put it into your own terms. The *product* you create, the actual pages of notes, give you a condensed version of the lesson that you can study later.

When you write every word exactly as the professor said it, you're just a conduit for the information, and it's less likely that any of it will stick in your brain. And 20 pages of notes may look impressive, but five are much easier to study!

Get Set: Preparing for Class & Managing Your Time

For today's college students, time management is more crucial than ever. In addition to your course loads, many of you are working at jobs—some of them full-time! Not to mention the internships, sports, volunteer work, and college events everyone wants you to participate in. To have a chance at juggling it all, you have to become a time-management expert.

The students who share their experiences in this chapter aren't pretending it all comes naturally to them. They are candid about the *special tricks and techniques they have had to come up with to stay on top of their many responsibilities. Check out what Natalee from Ohio and Vanessa from D.C. share about planning the whole semester based on the syllabi they get the first week. If you're new to college, this may seem like overkill, but believe me, it's not!*

You'll want to adapt for yourself some of the ideas you find here. And you will notice that one size definitely does not fit all. Be bold— try a few different techniques. The only technique you shouldn't try is no technique at all. Organize, experiment, explore: Soon you'll be managing your time so well that you'll walk into each class feeling rested, prepared, and confident. Or, at least, carrying the right text-book and having a pretty good idea of what it says.

IF YOU WANT TO BE PREPARED for class, print out the professor's notes. Our teachers post their notes online ahead of time. They are just bullet points on the lecture, but I like to print them out, read the corresponding text, and take a few notes on my own before class.

—LESLIE ROBINSON
LOS ANGELES, CALIFORNIA
UNIVERSITY OF CALIFORNIA, LOS ANGELES

• • • • • • • •

I KEEP MY BOOKS ORGANIZED on a shelf in my dorm room so that the ones for my next class are always on top. That way they're easy to grab before each class, and I don't have to stress about finding everything I need.

—DAWN RICHEY
RIPLEY, OHIO
XAVIER UNIVERSITY

• • • • • • • •

BEING ORGANIZED IS SO IMPORTANT: It can make or break you. The more organized you are, the more responsibilities you can take on and the more things you can accomplish. My freshman year, I read every page my teacher told me to. Soon I realized the magnitude of this attempt. My cousin told me once, "You don't have to read everything." It's true. In order to function in college, you can't read everything. That's where priorities come into play.

—LAURA GLASS
GOLDEN VALLEY, MINNESOTA
MINNESOTA UNIVERSITY OF ST. THOMAS

On weekends, prepare for your Monday and Tuesday classes; then on Monday you can just do that day's homework.

—CARRIE-LYNN
HODGE
MELBOURNE,
FLORIDA
WASHINGTON
UNIVERSITY IN
ST. LOUIS

KNOW YOUR CRITERIA

If your goal is to get the best grade possible, understand the criteria. For example, if the grade is based on exams, then the most important thing is to prepare for exams. If it's class participation, be prepared to participate. The teacher should state the criteria at the beginning of term, but if not, ask directly. People make a big mistake in this: They'd talk their heads off in class, and it would turn out that the grade was based 90 percent on a paper we turned in at the end. I remember a roommate spending day after day on a paper for a class, only to find out that the paper would comprise 5 percent of the grade at the end of the semester. She was furious, but could have avoided the aggravation had she just read the syllabus!

—JANE
MONTCLAIR, NEW JERSEY
BARNARD COLLEGE

GET TO KNOW YOUR CLASSMATES. You can get notes from them if you miss a class, call with any questions about class material, and study with them the long night before the test. Having friends in your classes also helps you keep your sanity; you can pass notes about the professor's crazy outfit, the party last night, or your weekend plans. My classmates are the friends I study with before tests and celebrate with after tests.

—LINDSEY JACKSON
LA GRANGE, GEORGIA
UNIVERSITY OF GEORGIA GPA: 3.9

• • • • • • • • •

USE YOUR FIRST FEW CLASSES to figure out what the assignments really mean. For example, the organic chemistry professor here might assign the first seven chapters of the textbook for reading, but it will turn out that the assignment is just a joke because he's covering everything that's in those chapters in the class.

—BEN
PASADENA, CALIFORNIA
CALIFORNIA INSTITUTE OF TECHNOLOGY GPA: 4

• • • • • • • • •

I TRY TO READ THE SECTION of the text before going to the class that will be covering the section. Usually, by the end of the semester, I get tired of doing this. Then I try to at least go over key points and words printed in bold.

—JODIE PIETRUCHA
MISHAWAKA, INDIANA
INDIANA UNIVERSITY, SOUTH BEND

WHY YOU REALLY DO NEED A PAPER PLANNER

One of the first things my advisees learn about me is that I am obsessed with time management—and, therefore, with planners. I believe in old-fashioned planners made of paper, small enough to be carried around in a backpack or purse.

"Why," many students ask, "do I need a planner, when I already put my appointments on my cell phone?" Other students love their computer calendars, or they just write everything on Post-it notes. And there are lots of other electronic gadgets that promise to help you organize every aspect of your life.

The truth as I see it: no other method or gadget is as truly useful as a paper planner. A planner won't crash or run out of battery power. You can flip through the pages of your planner and get a sense of what activities and deadlines are coming up. You can clip appointment cards and party invitations to the correct day, which takes even less time than typing the information into your PDA. And remember to hold on to your old yearly planners—they'll come in handy if you want to write your memoirs someday!

When I taught Developing Academic Success, I often took attendance by asking students to hold up their planners (a required item for the course) as I called their names. I wanted to reinforce the importance of keeping their time-management tool with them every day. Some of my students were annoyed by this at first, but once they started to reap the benefits of good time management, the complaints died down. Sometimes I would run into former students around campus, and they would pull out their planners and say, "See? I can't do without it now!"

Why does having (and using!) a planner make such a big difference? To see whether a planner would help you, ask yourself a few questions: "Do I ever miss appointments? Do I end up rushing to finish assignments at the last minute? Do I feel stressed out from trying to remember all the things I have to do? Do I often feel like I'm falling behind?"

If you answer "yes" to any of those questions, why not give yourself some help? Your life is much too complicated to run without a memory aid.

As I said before, your planner should fit easily into your backpack or purse. It should have a full page for each day, with sufficient space to mark down both time-specific commitments and general to-do lists.

If you aren't used to it, the initial task of putting all your commitments and deadlines into a planner may seem like a lot of work. But I'll bet that if you give it a try for one semester, you'll be hooked, too.

HARD AS IT MAY BE, try to get some sleep before class. Otherwise, unfortunate fashion mishaps may occur. One time in biology class, as I put my feet up on the back of the chair in front of me to get a little more comfortable, I realized that I was wearing two entirely different shoes. But honestly, I was so proud of myself for having made it to class that it almost didn't matter.

—KAROLINA SWIADEK
ARLINGTON, VIRGINIA

• • • • • • • •

The busier I am, the better I manage my time because there is no room to sit in front of my computer and go on facebook.com for hours and hours.

—MAGGIE
NEW YORK, NEW YORK
BROWN UNIVERSITY

• • • • • • • •

SOME PEOPLE WILL DO whatever is assigned to them; others will just blow things off and try to do the minimum necessary. I think both ways are bad. It's important to figure out what you must do to succeed in each course.

—BEN
PASADENA, CALIFORNIA
CALIFORNIA INSTITUTE OF TECHNOLOGY GPA: 4

WHEN READING AN ASSIGNMENT, look at the first and last sentences of a paragraph, if they are relevant to what you are studying, then read the whole thing; otherwise move on. You don't have to read every single page of every single assignment, just get the gist of it. I work 30 hours a week and I'm a full-time student, so I really had to learn about time management.

—MARIA CARMEL ROMANO
SAN DIEGO, CALIFORNIA
UNIVERSITY OF CALIFORNIA, SAN DIEGO

• • • • • • • •

COFFEE IN THE MORNING always helps give me a much-needed boost for class. I also go online and print out my professors' PowerPoint presentations. Bringing the print-outs to class means I don't have to write down everything, and it gives me a place to add key concepts and extra details that help me understand the material.

—VANESSA HOFFMAN
WASHINGTON, D.C.
CORNELL UNIVERSITY

• • • • • • • •

TAKE SERIOUSLY THE AMOUNT OF TIME your professor tells you to put into a class. During the first week of each class, your professor might say, "This class will require ten hours of outside work." Make sure you put that much time into your studies.

Consider

—MICHAEL POWELL
GLENDALE, CALIFORNIA
UNIVERSITY OF CALIFORNIA, BERKELEY GPA: 3.63

I ALWAYS KEEP MY DESK really clean; if I have a lot of stuff on it, I will not work. I always keep my notebook really nice too. When I'm disorganized I just don't work well.

—ANONYMOUS
BARRINGTON, ILLINOIS
UNIVERSITY OF CALIFORNIA, LOS ANGELES

* * * * * * * *

IT ALL COMES DOWN TO ORGANIZATION and common sense. I found that the key to getting everything done and not procrastinating was just writing down everything I had to do every week. And I mean *everything*. If I had to get groceries or return a book to the library or go to the bank, it went on the list right next to studying for a midterm or interviewing the president of the university for a news article. Then the next step is organizing it in terms of importance: I had a good system of Post-it notes going.

—ANDREW SHAFER
NEW YORK, NEW YORK
IOWA STATE UNIVERSITY GPA: 3.34

* * * * * * * *

I TOOK A CLASS AND DIDN'T STUDY that much. I did poorly on the midterm, so that motivated me to study really hard so I could do well on the final. I ended up getting the same grade on the final that I got on my midterm. I realized that you can't just jump in midway; you have to start from the beginning.

—CURTIS
MISSION VIEJO, CALIFORNIA

> I got work-study jobs where I could read while I was working. That killed two birds with one stone.
>
> —JASON BRUNER
> CARTERSVILLE, GEORGIA
> GARDNER-WEBB UNIVERSITY

GOT HELP?

THE WAY TO SUCCEED IS TO GET HELP; I think wanting to do well is the most important thing I was in a psych course that had a lot to do with formulas; I just wasn't that interested in it. I had another exam that week that I was studying for, and since the professor in the psych course told us that he'd drop our lowest exam score, I didn't even study for the first quiz. It made a bad impression, and my professor was really hard on me. He said, "To say you did poorly would be the understatement of the century." After that, I went straight to my TA and said, "Help!" I did well in the course, by the end.

—A.K.
POUND RIDGE, NEW YORK
BOSTON COLLEGE

• • • • • • • •

I WISH I HAD GONE TO MORE OFFICE HOURS. I'm kind of a procrastinator when it comes to studying so I never had any questions, but I would still go to office hours and just listen to other people ask questions; I would learn a lot. People would ask the professor to go over concepts or slides again. I'd been told when I was a freshman of the importance of going to office hours but I didn't end up going until senior year.

—ANONYMOUS
IRVINE, CALIFORNIA
UNIVERSITY OF CALIFORNIA, LOS ANGELES

WHEN I SIT DOWN TO READ, I highlight what I think is important and I write notes in the margins. That way, when I'm sitting in class later and my professor starts talking about part of the text, I can find it easily because I have highlighted it.

—JANET WU
CARY, NORTH CAROLINA
DUKE UNIVERSITY

• • • • • • • •

THE PROFESSORS TREAT YOU like big kids and expect you to read. If you don't read, you don't learn as much, and you're not getting your own enjoyment or money's worth out of the class. Read: It's simple but it's quite effective.

—NED
NEW ORLEANS, LOUISIANA
YALE UNIVERSITY

• • • • • • • •

IT'S JUST NOT POSSIBLE to read 50 to100 pages a night for each class. I make things easier on myself by spending a couple of weeks figuring out how my professor works. If I learn that certain reading assignments will only be talked about in class and won't be tested, I read some of the beginning, some of the middle, and some of the end of the assignment so I'll know enough to participate in the discussion.

—JASON PAUL TORREANO
LOCKPORT, NEW YORK
STATE UNIVERSITY OF NEW YORK, BROCKPORT

ONE OF THE SIMPLEST THINGS that I did was to keep a detailed planner. I wrote every assignment, every test, every meeting and every due date in it. During the first week of class, I entered important dates into my planner from each professor's syllabus. I could never forget that a paper was due or that I had a test because it was staring at me from the pages of my planner.

—NATALEE
MARTINS FERRY, OHIO
XAVIER UNIVERSITY

* * * * * * * *

AT THE BEGINNING OF THE SEMESTER I take the class syllabus and write down all of my assignments, exams and projects in a daily planner. Once I finish something, such as a reading assignment, I check it off on the syllabus. It's a little thing, but making those check marks makes me feel that I'm accomplishing something every day.

—VANESSA HOFFMAN
WASHINGTON, D.C.
CORNELL UNIVERSITY

* * * * * * * *

GET YOUR HOMEWORK DONE before anything else. My first semester of my freshman year, I didn't even join clubs because I wanted to see how much time it would take me to get homework done. Now, I know how much time it takes and I have extra time to do what I want. Last night, I went out and had a blast.

—JON WALDO
NASHVILLE, TENNESSEE
BOSTON UNIVERSITY

The busier you are, the more productive you'll be with the time you have left over.

—D.N.M.
SEATTLE,
WASHINGTON
WASHINGTON
UNIVERSITY

I USE COLOR CODING on my Palm Pilot. For instance, anything to do with my internship is navy blue; family is lavender blue; travel is orange; friends are aqua-green; my sorority is yellow. That way, I just look at my daily calendar, and even if I don't have time to read everything that's going on, I just see colors and think, "Oh my God, what's going on with my internship this afternoon?" Colors really stick out.

—ELEANOR W. HAND
ATLANTA, GEORGIA
UNIVERSITY OF GEORGIA

I prepared for class every morning by reading a chapter ahead of what would be discussed.

—WANJIRU
CARBONDALE,
ILLINOIS
ILLINOIS
UNIVERSITY,
CARBONDALE

IF YOU ARE THE TYPE OF PERSON who can comprehend and remember everything the professor says in his lecture, then you can slack off on the reading a bit. Most of the professors here write their own textbooks, so obviously they will be lifting right from the book in the lecture. I used to cram, cram, cram on the reading. Eventually I realized that what I was reading was exactly what they were talking about in class, so I pulled back a little and I am still getting A's.

—J.T.
BURBANK, CALIFORNIA
UNIVERSITY OF CALIFORNIA, LOS ANGELES GPA: 3.3

I'M A DANCER and an architecture student, and it works well for me to do my architecture work right after I finish dancing. It gets my adrenaline and my mind going.

—ALEX J. GORDON
CHINA, TEXAS
WASHINGTON UNIVERSITY

IT SOUNDS COUNTERINTUITIVE, but get involved with a lot of things, and you'll use your time more wisely. I'm into art and playing music, and I'm in a student coop; it all helps me to plan my time better.

—S.S.
CURLEW, WASHINGTON
WASHINGTON UNIVERSITY IN ST. LOUIS

• • • • • • • •

Your class syllabus can do a lot to help keep you prepared. Don't just stuff it in a folder: Check it regularly to make sure you're on top of everything.

—DAWN RICHEY
RIPLEY, OHIO
XAVIER UNIVERSITY

• • • • • • • •

SINCE I ALWAYS HAD A PART-TIME, ON-CAMPUS JOB, and was heavily involved in student organizations, I knew time management was key to having good grades. I scheduled most of my classes in the morning. After class, I would come home and study for a few hours until work. Afterwards, I made sure I got some rest, and when the weekend came it was time to party.

—MICHAEL BAKER
AURORA, ILLINOIS
BENEDICTINE UNIVERSITY

HOW TO READ A TEXTBOOK

Open your textbook. Read the chapter from beginning to end. Close the book. What's wrong with this technique? Everything! You can put in a lot of time and good, earnest effort studying this way. Time and effort should equal learning and sometimes do, but not in this case. To really get the textbook material you have to read actively. The Survey-Question-Write-Read-Recite-Review Method can help you.

SURVEY: Skim through your chapter and get a general sense of what it's about. Highlight the title and section headings.

QUESTION: Ask yourself, "What do I want to get from this chapter? What do I need to learn?"

WRITE: Compose your own study questions. Now your goal is to answer them.

READ: As you work your way through, look for the information you need.

RECITE: Impress the information even further upon your memory by saying it out loud.

REVIEW: Now that you have written study questions and answers, you can review these "reading notes" easily before or after class. This is much easier than slogging through all the textbook chapters again and again!

I WRITE DOWN MY ASSIGNMENTS and schedule my week on a spreadsheet so I can get as much work done during the day as possible and I don't get stuck doing everything at night. If I don't plan it out ahead of time, I can easily squander an hour in between classes rather than get an assignment out of the way. My schedule also allows me to go out on the weekends. If I get my work done during the day, I can go out without guilt on a Thursday or Friday night.

—NAOMI GOLDIN
HAWTHORNE, NEW YORK
CORNELL UNIVERSITY GPA: 3.59

* * * * * * * *

DURING MY FIRST SEMESTER, I took class notes by hand and that same night I typed them up into a word document. That reinforcement helped the information sink in.

—DAVID SCHWARTZ
CHATTANOOGA, TENNESSEE
WASHINGTON UNIVERSITY GPA: 3.6

* * * * * * * *

I BOUGHT MY OWN ROLLING DESK CHAIR with arms and a headrest, instead of using the dorm-provided chair. With a good desk chair studying became a much easier, less painful task. Plus, it's more attractive, less awkward, and takes up less space in my room. When living in the dorms, space becomes a precious commodity.

—BRITTANY
DALLAS, TEXAS
UNIVERSITY OF OKLAHOMA GPA: 4

I gave myself eight hours of sleep each night.

—CHANA
SERGEANT
CHICAGO,
ILLINOIS
NORTHERN
ILLINOIS
UNIVERSITY

SET ASIDE THINGS you want to do for a certain time period: This is when I do my reading; this is when I do my papers. I normally do a little work in the morning before class. Most of my studying happens in the afternoon and evening.

—NED
NEW ORLEANS, LOUISIANA
YALE UNIVERSITY

• • • • • • • •

Calendars and planners are too bulky. I get it all done by writing out my schedule for the week on a piece of paper or on a note card.

—JANET WU
CARY, NORTH CAROLINA
DUKE UNIVERSITY

• • • • • • • •

I THINK IT'S DEFINITELY A GOOD IDEA to get things done ahead of time. You'll be more rested going into the next day. On the other hand, if the weather is gorgeous, be willing to sacrifice some of your evening to be outside during the day.

—ELIZABETH
MOORESTOWN, NEW JERSEY
FAIRFIELD UNIVERSITY

DON'T LISTEN TO MUSIC when you study; it just distracts you. I hear so many people say, "I just have to do two things at once." You think you are getting more done, but it's much more productive if you focus completely and only on your books.

—CYNTHIA KOSSAYAN
LA CRESCENTA, CALIFORNIA
UNIVERSITY OF CALIFORNIA, LOS ANGELES GPA: 3.5

• • • • • • • •

I MADE A PLAN: I would devote so many hours to an activity. I participated in a sorority that took up most of my time. On top of that, I was taking 15 credits, a full load. I also belonged to another outside group, PRSSA (Public Relations Society of America) and I was part of the Puppy Sitter Club, for seeing-eye dogs if their owners needed a break. It was hard. You have to juggle study and extracurricular activities. A planner really works for organizing it all.

—ELIZABETH ANNE ALARIO
WARREN, NEW JERSEY
RUTGERS UNIVERSITY

• • • • • • • •

DISTRACTIONS COME FROM EVERYWHERE; the computer that you use to write papers is the same one you use to read your e-mail and chat with your friends. Force yourself to set time to study and ignore distractions, even if it takes booby-trapping your dorm-room door.

—ALMOG VIDAVSKY
ST. LOUIS, MISSOURI
WASHINGTON UNIVERSITY IN ST. LOUIS

WHERE DOES THE TIME REALLY GO? BE HONEST.

If you take an orientation or college skills course, you'll probably do one of those time management exercises where you fill in a chart with all your activities, quarter-hour by quarter-hour. And if you are like 90 percent of college students, you'll find this exercise a bit tedious (the other 10 percent enjoy it because filling in activities with different colors appeals to their artistic side.)

Of all the orientation/college skills assignments I've seen over the years, this one inspires the most resistance—the first time around. But a funny thing happens as students get a little further in their college experience. Often when a student takes a second course that requires this exercise, or simply makes a chart because his advisor suggested it, he discovers something strange: our time doesn't always go where we think it's going.

In high school, things were simpler: school during the day, maybe extracurricular activities in the afternoon, studying in the evening, dinner, probably some TV or Internet time, then bed. Perhaps you also had a job. Those hours were likely fairly regular too. But in college your Mondays could be completely different from your Tuesdays—and next semester everything changes again. You have three hours between Organic Chemistry and

Sociology that just seem to disappear. On Thursdays you don't have class until 1 p.m., so that morning is supposed to be your time to catch up, but somehow you don't *feel* caught up.

When you analyze the patterns of time use that appear on your chart, you can decide (if you need to) to make some changes. Is your commute taking longer than it has to because you are driving during rush hour? Are you using breaks between classes to the best advantage? How much time do you spend doing non-academic stuff on the computer? How much time do you spend on the phone with your parents, or your best friend back home, or your significant other at another college three states away?

In my opinion, money is important, but it is still not quite up there in importance with time. Just as you keep track of your finances, make sure that you are spending your time on the right activities and staying out of debt. If you learn this lesson in college, you will be ahead of the game when you go out into the real world.

WATCH YOUR TIME. Dining hall, for example, can sometimes interfere with studying. It's really easy to talk to a lot of people and stay there forever. The conversations are good on one level: You have great conversations with fellow students, and I even got an idea for a paper from one heated discussion we were having. But then you check your watch and realize you've been there two hours instead of the 20 minutes you'd planned on.

—ANNA
PRINCETON, NEW JERSEY
PRINCETON UNIVERSITY

. . . .

When the weekend rolls around and I get the urge to relax, I tell myself that if I get a certain amount of work done, I can treat myself later that night.

—K.O.
LOS ANGELES, CALIFORNIA
EMORY UNIVERSITY

. . . .

SOMETIMES I'LL END UP WASTING TIME in the stupidest ways—running back and forth from the store buying drinks, for example.

—NICK
LOS ANGELES, CALIFORNIA
YALE UNIVERSITY

A Sense of Place: Where to Study & What to Eat

I am in a great mood as I write this chapter introduction because one of my advisees just told me she has finally tried studying in the library—and she loves it. This student, Yolanda, insisted for months that she could only get her work done at home.

Unfortunately, home was two hours away. So much of Yolanda's time was taken up by commuting, little time and no energy were left for studying. It took a lot of effort for her to break out of her familiar pattern, but she did, and she is reaping the benefits. I'm so happy about it, I don't even mind that after all my gentle suggestions that

Yolanda try the college library, what did the trick was her friend pointing out a particular quiet floor.

Consider the students in this chapter to be your *friends, pointing out good study spots to you. Be adventurous and voyage outside your comfort zone. See what happens!*

I WAS ON ACADEMIC PROBATION. I spoke to a friend who told me: go to the library two hours a night; limit the distractions; in the library, be by yourself or with a study partner. In the library, you can get 50 minutes of quality time out of an hour, versus 20 minutes in front of a television or computer. My first three semesters were horrible, but the final four semesters, in my major, I had a 3.4 GPA.

> —NICK
> NEW CITY, NEW YORK
> UNIVERSITY OF MICHIGAN

MY WORST STUDY MISTAKE was getting together with a group of friends—with different study habits—and trying to learn material the night before an exam. I wasted a lot of time trying to adjust to everybody's version of how to learn. Study with just one other person whom you know you work well with; any more can be too distracting!

> —A.S.
> NEW YORK, NEW YORK
> QUEEN'S UNIVERSITY

STUDYING AT HOME means I'll be most comfortable, but when I need to really crack down I find a quiet spot in the library or a bookstore. Sometimes you need to be away from any possible distraction.

> —A.S.
> CHICAGO, ILLINOIS
> UNIVERSITY OF WISCONSIN

I WISH I HAD DISCOVERED a secret study spot. My whole college career, I have always studied in my room, while sitting on my bed (which, I have been reminded numerous times, is the worst place to study). Finding a comfortable place to sit and study is important because you will most likely be there awhile.

—RACHEL ALDRICH
BROOKLYN PARK, MINNESOTA
UNIVERSITY OF WISCONSIN GPA: 3.7

• • • • • • • •

I WOULD GO TO COFFEE SHOPS and to the school library to get in some quiet time. I also utilized the library at a nearby law school because it was even more quiet and comfortable. If I needed to cram for a test I would go to Denny's, sit in a back booth, and work on a pot of coffee.

—LEIGH
CHICAGO, ILLINOIS
WESLEYAN UNIVERSITY

• • • • • • • •

I FOUND ONE OR TWO PLACES on campus that felt comfortable and were out of the main path of traffic. The history building has beautiful wood and huge windowsills; I used to climb up on one and study while looking at the garden in the back. My other spot was the first floor of the library, where they had a row of study carrels. I could plug in my computer and hunker down, but I could still crane my neck up and see what was going on around me if I wanted to.

—H.D.
WESTIN, CONNECTICUT
SWARTHMORE COLLEGE

A BOUQUET OF STUDY TIPS

- Don't try to study while watching TV.
- Don't study on your bed; you will only end up falling asleep.
- Find a quiet place, away from your friends who will distract you.
- Listen to instrumental music on an iPod. It helps to drown out distracting conversations and noises and does not have lyrics that you will want to sing along with.
- Turn off your cell phone or you will be tempted to procrastinate by sending text messages.

—LINDSEY JACKSON
LA GRANGE, GEORGIA
UNIVERSITY OF GEORGIA GPA: 3.9

I HAVE A REALLY SMALL DESK, and everyone makes fun of me because it's so small. No one understands, though, that the less space you have, the less clutter you will accumulate; when you don't have clutter, you are more productive.

—CYNTHIA KOSSAYAN
LA CRESCENTA, CALIFORNIA
UNIVERSITY OF CALIFORNIA, LOS ANGELES GPA: 3.5

CELL PHONE MANNERS

Can you believe that there was a time when no one had cell phones? Today, you probably have a cell phone and can't imagine being without it. To prevent it from hindering your academic success, though, take my advice:

- Don't answer your phone in any academic setting. This includes the classroom, the tutoring center, the library, and your academic advisor's office. I have watched, my mouth hanging open in shock, as students not only answered their cell phones in the middle of an appointment with me, but went on to have a little chat with the caller! You don't want to be that kid.

- Don't set your ringer to "vibrate" or "silent," because it's not; I can always hear it. And if it happens to be sitting on a hard surface like a desk or table, it really rattles, sometimes lurching around like a metallic hermit crab. Don't draw your professor's ire: turn your cell phone *all* the way off.

- Keep your voice down when you're on your cell phone, even if you're in a public space like the quad or the dining hall. Okay, maybe this one isn't as relevant to academic success—it's more a general call for civility. But won't we all be more successful if we're less distracted and annoyed by noise?

STAY ON THE MOVE! I couldn't just sit and read textbooks for hours on end, so my weekend study method would begin at about 8 a.m. every Saturday at a nearby coffee shop. I would order coffee and a bagel and proceed to plow through chapter after chapter. After about two hours, I would go for a walk or a drive for about 30 minutes and then head to the next study location—another coffee shop or a local library. I'd repeat this process until about 7 or 8 p.m., then collapse.

—CINDY
ST. LOUIS, MISSOURI
🏛 WASHINGTON UNIVERSITY IN ST. LOUIS

I have a better GPA since I've cut back on soda!

—MICHAEL ABRAMOVITZ
ALTA LOMA, CALIFORNIA
🏛 UNIVERSITY OF ARIZONA
GPA: 2.65

* * * * * * * *

I HAD TO AVOID STUDYING in the library because they had a really awesome film collection and rooms you could watch them in. Often I would just wind up watching these movies instead of studying.

—RAFAEL
HONG KONG, CHINA
🏛 GEORGETOWN UNIVERSITY GPA: 3.4

* * * * * * * *

I EAT A LOT OF CEREAL when I'm studying. I eat it straight out of the box, and the sugar keeps me awake.

—J.A.
BOSTON, MASSACHUSETTS
🏛 UNIVERSITY OF SOUTHERN CALIFORNIA GPA: 3.8

THE QUEEN RECOMMENDS

In college I was known as the queen of all-nighters. I developed a full arsenal of tools to stay awake and coherent beyond the powers of most mortals. Here, in a nutshell, are the most powerful tools I know for staying energized and sane:

- Ginseng is a plant that gives long-term energy without the same kind of crash as caffeine. You can get it as a tea or as a juice, or you can get sliced ginseng in honey at most Asian food stores.
- Emergen-C is a magic product that's essentially all the vitamins you need in powder form. It gives you energy, keeps you awake, and it also keeps you from getting sick.
- Echinacea tea is a godsend for staying healthy when everyone around you is sick.

—LAURA CARROLL
SALEM, MASSACHUSETTS

OBVIOUSLY FRUITS AND VEGGIES will make you feel healthier; but let's be honest: few of us crave that when we're working hard! You also don't want to eat anything with too much garlic, onions, or salt because an hour or two later, you'll feel yucky. I like to snack on tea biscuits, grapes, pretzels, and granola when I'm working late. I also used to put a few hard-boiled eggs in my mini fridge and eat those as a snack.

—A.S.
NEW YORK, NEW YORK
QUEEN'S UNIVERSITY

Take your laptop to the computer lab or library. Having people around you working will make you work longer and harder.

—NINA
SAN FRANCISCO, CALIFORNIA
UNIVERSITY OF WASHINGTON GPA: 3.4

THE LIBRARY WAS MY REFUGE in time of trouble. If I knew my friends were on their way to my dorm to ask me to party the day before an assignment was due, I would run to the top floor of the library, in the corner of the nearly empty place. Nobody would think to look for me there.

—ANONYMOUS
CHICAGO, ILLINOIS

I ALWAYS HATED STUDYING in the library. All those people working quietly; it was really distracting. I always found that studying somewhere with a little noise—the student union, a coffee shop—was more relaxing because it kind of tricked my mind into thinking it wasn't studying.

—DANIEL
NEW YORK, NEW YORK
UNIVERSITY OF PENNSYLVANIA GPA: 3.7

• • • • • • • •

MY SECRET STUDY SPOT is at a local coffee shop called A Fine Grind. This little cafe is usually full of students I have classes with, so I can ask them questions if I need to. It's a little walk from where I live, but that gives me time to nail down what I need to do and in what order it needs to be done. The atmosphere is very relaxed, with quiet music playing and the smell of coffee in the air.

—BRIDGET SCRABECK
LAKEVILLE, MINNESOTA
UNIVERSITY OF ST. THOMAS

• • • • • • • •

I LIKE TO STUDY between the bookshelves in the library. Wherever I find the book I'm looking for is right where I will usually grab a seat. I'm the type of person who needs total quiet to study; even the sound of a computer keyboard distracts me. Since laptops are everywhere I need to work hard to find that special spot where I can really be alone.

—J.T.
BURBANK, CALIFORNIA
UNIVERSITY OF CALIFORNIA, LOS ANGELES GPA: 3.3

BEST STUDY FOOD EVER!

BEN & JERRY'S ICE CREAM. But not so great for battling the Freshman 15!

> —REBECCA
> WASHINGTON, D.C.

• • • • • • • •

GOLDFISH, PIZZA, and s'mores that you make in your microwave in your room. You get the satisfaction of salty, sweet, and cheesy.

> —ERICA
> HOUSTON, TEXAS
> SYRACUSE UNIVERSITY GPA: 3.3

• • • • • • • •

WATER. HYDRATION IS A GREAT THING—and going to the bathroom later provides a fabulous pee break.

> —NICOLE SPENCE
> ATLANTA, GEORGIA
> EMORY UNIVERSITY GPA: 3.71

• • • • • • • •

SWEDISH FISH! You have to chew them or else you'll choke on your saliva, so it keeps you awake.

> —LISA FREEDMAN
> NEW YORK, NEW YORK

IF YOU HAVE A PROJECT that requires uninterrupted silence, be sure to check out your school's law library, as long as it's near campus and allows access to undergraduates. Somewhere along the way, the same law students who hog airtime in undergraduate lectures turn into soulless drones obsessed with case studies who embrace silence. This combination provides a perfect, soundless location for you to focus. A nice change from the main library, which is primarily populated by freshmen with no better place to socialize.

—SAM WEAVER
MINNEAPOLIS, MINNESOTA
MARQUETTE UNIVERSITY

I ALWAYS STUDIED IN THE ENGINEERING building's student lounge from 4 p.m. until 9 p.m., Monday through Friday. I would take my dinner and heat it up in their microwave, so I would have no reason to leave my study area.

—CORAVIECE TERRY
MOUNDS, ILLINOIS
SOUTHERN ILLINOIS UNIVERSITY, CARBONDALE

MY FAVORITE PLACE TO STUDY was Starbucks. Their stores had long tables, so I'd set out all my books and study several subjects at once. I would stock up on coffee, and they wouldn't kick me out until it was time to close.

—KENDRA GONZALEZ
SCHAUMBURG, ILLINOIS
UNIVERSITY OF ILLINOIS

YOUR IDEAL ENVIRONMENT

As you can see in this chapter, everyone is different. Some students can't imagine studying in a coffee shop while others swear by it. Some students love the library; for others, all that quiet is creepy! To make sure your intended study space is the best place for you to learn, first think about your preferences:

- Noisy, muted noise, or dead quiet? (Note: most people are distracted by recognizable language— TV, song lyrics, and nearby conversation.)
- Public space or private room?
- Crowded or empty?
- Warm or cool?
- Dim or brightly lit?
- A familiar corner of the library, or a new place every time?
- Facing a window with a pretty view that refreshes you, or facing a wall that is so plain and boring your least favorite textbook seems fascinating by comparison?

OUR FIR (FACULTY-IN-RESIDENCE) will have Study Break, a night where they provide refreshments in their living room. The best Study Break consisted of delicious breakfast foods, including regular and chocolate-chip pancakes with syrup and whipped cream, sausage and bacon, fruit, coffee, and juice. It was exactly what we needed to regain our concentration for studying!

—BRITTANY
DALLAS, TEXAS
UNIVERSITY OF OKLAHOMA GPA: 4

I considered studying a part-time job and my weekly salary was a passing grade, and a bonus would be making the Dean's List, which I accomplished once.

—T.C.
PRAIRIE DU CHIEN, WISCONSIN
UNIVERSITY OF WISCONSIN

POPCORN IS A GOOD STUDY SNACK because you don't feel heavy when you're finished and it lasts a long time. You don't want heavy carbs or sugar that will make you want to go to sleep.

—VERONICA
TORONTO, CANADA
CASE WESTERN RESERVE UNIVERSITY

I DON'T BUY THE IDEA that people can really be productive leaning up against a tree with uncoordinated people throwing Frisbees and footballs around them. Not to mention, in the springtime, when the freshman girls who don't know any better are wearing short skirts, can any male not have his head on a swivel? And please, in a coffee shop—the grinding of the coffee beans, employees making smoothies and lattes, people walking in and out smelling of cigarettes; I guess some people may find it a peaceful place to get some work done.

—TOM M. NEMO
OAKDALE, MINNESOTA
UNIVERSITY OF MINNESOTA

I LIKE TO STUDY NEAR PEOPLE, in the library or student lounge, but not necessarily in a study group. Alone in my dorm room, it is too tempting to turn on the television, listen to the radio, talk on the phone, or visit a friend in another room. Being near other people who are serious about studying keeps me on my toes.

—KANEDA IRVIN
CHICAGO, ILLINOIS
SOUTHERN ILLINOIS UNIVERSITY, CARBONDALE

I LIKE TO STUDY WITH LIFE cereal because I can snack on it easily, I don't need milk with it, and it's not greasy, like potato chips.

—MARIA
MORAGO, CALIFORNIA
STANFORD UNIVERSITY

FIVE WAYS TO STOP STUDYING ON YOUR BED

The jury is in, and the verdict is clear: the worst possible place to study is your bed. Apart from the obvious danger of falling asleep, there are numerous reasons to find a study spot far away from your cozy mattress, pillows, and blankets. For one thing, your lap probably doesn't give you the surface area you need for your books, notebook, highlighters, index cards, dictionary, and so forth. For another, if your friends walk in and see you in a reclining pose, even if you're holding a book, they'll probably think, "Oh, s/he's not *really* working. There's no harm in tempting him/her with a quick game of Wii bowling."

And yet, it's so easy to convince yourself that this time you'll stay awake and get some serious studying done. Instead, trick yourself with one of these methods:

1. If you live in a dorm and have a mini fridge, keep the mini fridge closer to your desk than it is to your bed. (Although in your average dorm room, everything is pretty close together anyway.)
2. Hang a "No Studying" sign over your bed.

3. Create a studying ritual for yourself at your desk, such as taking a lucky penny or other special object out of your desk drawer every time you hit the books. Soon, your brain will associate studying with that location above all others.

4. If you have a roommate (or two), see if they'll join you in a "No Studying On the Bed" pact. Then be strict with each other.

5. If none of these ideas work, then for goodness' sake, grab your book bag and head for the library!

CARROTS AND HUMMUS ARE GREAT to eat while studying because they don't make you feel yucky, and thinking while chewing has always worked for me. The protein in hummus gives you a little boost, too.

—MICHAEL PAOLI
NEW YORK, NEW YORK
UNIVERSITY OF TORONTO GPA: 3.4

• • • • • • • •

I used to study in the library until I realized that lack of oxygen and fresh air made me delirious.

—JULIE
BEVERLY HILLS, CALIFORNIA
UNIVERSITY OF SOUTHERN CALIFORNIA GPA: 3.4

I WAS STUDYING WITH A GIRL for a history exam and we ordered chicken wings. We got our food and she taught me everything while I ate. As long as you have something to make it enjoyable, you'll forget that you're studying.

—JOE
NEW MILFORD, CONNECTICUT
UNIVERSITY OF CONNECTICUT GPA: 3

• • • • • • • •

I SWEAR BY BANANAS WHEN STUDYING. You don't want food that is going to be greasy and heavy in your stomach.

—JESSE MCCREE
SOMERVILLE, MASSACHUSETTS
BOWDOIN COLLEGE GPA: 3.6

• • • • • • • •

THE BEST THING TO EAT while you are studying is peanut butter and crackers. The protein in the peanut butter gives you energy. It's also really filling, so you don't eat too much of it.

—S.A.
FRAMINGHAM, MASSACHUSETTS
UNIVERSITY OF SOUTHERN CALIFORNIA GPA: 3.6

DO IT IN A GROUP

For study groups keep these considerations in mind:

FRIENDS OR NON-FRIENDS? You may be much more motivated to show up for your study group if it means hanging out with your favorite people. Be sure, however, that your group is able to stay on task. If your meetings are 90 percent socialization, something has to change.

HIGHER, EQUAL, OR LOWER? Studying with higher-level students can inspire you to stretch yourself. But it can be discouraging if everyone in your group is learning faster and earning higher grades. Look for a group of students who are approximately at your level; for this purpose, it's good to be average!

CLOSING CEREMONIES? Many study groups conclude their sessions with dinner, hot chocolate, and so forth. Just make sure that your reward for studying is not canceling out the studying. I once worked with some students who reported putting in quite a few hours in their study group without getting the results they wanted. Eventually they revealed that they celebrated the end of each study session by smoking marijuana. Getting high immediately after studying complex scientific concepts was probably not a good way to retain the information!

WHAT'S YOUR PRIME TIME?

There's a stereotype that every college student likes to stay up all night and sleep all day. Of course, there are some nights when you stay up, and they are usually followed by days when you sleep. This doesn't mean, however, that late nights are necessarily your "prime" time.

When I first taught Developing Academic Success, my university's tutorial center coordinator, Julianne Scibetta, would come in to do an exercise with the students. By asking them when they felt most awake and alert, when they had energy, and when they were focused, she helped them identify their key time or times of day. Early morning, late morning, afternoon, evening, or night—what some of the students found out surprised them!

Once you've figured out your prime time, you can plan your life around that knowledge. Schedule your hardest class at a time when your mind is most ready to learn. If you have a break during your prime time, use it to brainstorm and make an outline for your 10-page paper or your five-minute presentation. And if your prime time happens when your roommate is asleep, just be considerate—when you figure out that tricky calculus problem or finally get that introductory paragraph just right, do all your cheering *inside* your head.

I RECOMMEND FRUIT, like apples, oranges, and grapes when studying. Not only are they tasty, but they are full of water which is critical, since hydration improves awareness and concentration.

> —SAMUEL
> PALO ALTO, CALIFORNIA
> STANFORD UNIVERSITY

* * * * * * * *

MY MOM USED TO SEND ME her homemade treats, like stuffed zucchini with rice and meat, and baklava. That worked well as a care package because it was fast, filling and reminded me of home. You need that sometimes when you're in the heart of studying!

> —MICHAEL PAOLI
> NEW YORK, NEW YORK
> UNIVERSITY OF TORONTO GPA: 3.4

* * * * * * * *

MY BEST FRIEND AND I EXISTED on chocolate-chip cookie dough each time we attempted to buckle down and write our English papers the night before they were due. In retrospect, I realize we could have given ourselves a deadly case of salmonella poisoning; the raw eggs in the batter can potentially kill you. But the sugar rush from the chocolate chips and the dough really helped us counteract the serious procrastination we suffered from when it came to writing papers.

> —STEVE
> SOUTH ORANGE, NEW JERSEY
> UNIVERSITY OF CALIFORNIA, RIVERSIDE GPA: 3.5

SUGAR IS ALWAYS A GOOD "UPPER" when you're studying. Just make sure you don't eat tons of it or you'll crash. Sometimes a little exercise to get the blood circulating can help, since most of us study sitting at a table. Alcohol is not a good option!

—ANONYMOUS
NEW YORK, NEW YORK

* * * * * * * *

Crunchy is key when you're studying. Crunchy foods always help keep me awake because they're so loud. When you chew it shakes you awake.

—AMANDA NELSON-DUAC
GRANBURY, TEXAS
GEORGE WASHINGTON UNIVERSITY GPA: 3.6

* * * * * * * *

FINDING THE PERFECT PLACE to study could make or break your semester. Try unconventional places where there won't be a lot of students. In my four years at Cornell, I've studied in stairwells, the stands of the basketball court, and parks. I often sneaked into classrooms after hours.

—JACOB SZE
ELLENVILLE, NEW YORK
CORNELL UNIVERSITY

YOUR REWARDS PROGRAM

You probably have many reasons for wanting to succeed in college, but what do you do when those goals seem far away and you just can't summon up much motivation to do your work in the here and now?

Bribe yourself: I do it every week. When I first started graduate school, I realized that going to night classes after a long day at the office would be a challenge. In addition, my commute to school involved two subway trains each way, plus a long, cold walk on the way home. I couldn't afford to miss class, but there would be nights when I would try to convince myself otherwise.

I decided to play to one of my weaknesses—my craving for the cheeseburgers and fries at a certain fast-food restaurant. Normally I try to maintain a healthy diet, but on the nights I go to class I allow myself a special stop on the way home. If I have participated in the class discussion, I get my cheeseburger. If I have participated a lot, I get fries, too. Guess what? In six semesters, I've barely missed a class, and I always find plenty to say.

Your reward may be something quite different—new music, a fruit smoothie at the campus center, half an hour off to watch some truly frivolous television show with your friends. The important thing is to only treat yourself to that particular reward when you've accomplished your task. No cheating! Your cheeseburger (or whatever you choose) will taste better when you've earned it.

I NEED CHOCOLATE CHIPS to help me with my studies. I always have a bag of them on hand. I know they are bad for my teeth, but they keep me up.

—NATHANIEL
PHILADELPHIA, PENNSYLVANIA
STANFORD UNIVERSITY GPA: 3.7

• • • • • • • •

I ALWAYS HAVE A SUPPLY OF JELLYBEANS, chocolate kisses, gummy bears and Sour Patch Kids. The taste of candy reminds me of being at home because my mom always had candy lying around the house. It also keeps me awake for hours.

—ANONYMOUS
NEW YORK, NEW YORK
LEHIGH UNIVERSITY

• • • • • • • •

I WOULD RECOMMEND ANY SORT of healthy foods to help with studying. Dried fruits and nuts are great. Apples, clementines, and yogurt are good study foods, too; they can be easily transported and preserved. Wheat Thins with string cheese or peanut butter is one of my favorites. Also, I love gummy fruit.

—BRITTANY
DALLAS, TEXAS
UNIVERSITY OF OKLAHOMA GPA: 4

Going the Distance: Tips on Writing a Good Paper

A friend of mine who, in years past, reigned as the king of online dating, told me how picky he was about what women on dating Web sites wrote in their profiles.

"Bad grammar, misspellings, malapropisms—all total deal-breakers." If a woman wrote "compliment" when she clearly meant "complement"—no date. If she wrote "mischievious" (incorrect) instead of "mischievous" (correct)—no date. I decided not to tell my friend about the college paper I wrote on E.M. Forster's novel

Howards End, *in which I accidentally got the title wrong throughout the paper (I called the book* Howard's End, *with the extra apostrophe.)*

This goes to show that good writing is important in all kinds of situations, and people will definitely judge you by how well you write.

As you'll read in this chapter, to end up with a great paper you have to start with solid ideas and build them up in a structure that makes sense. To switch metaphors, think of your paper as an oil painting, not a watercolor. In watercolors, the artist has one chance to get it right, because going back over the brush strokes ruins the clarity of the colors. Luckily, you don't have to get your papers perfect in one draft! Oil paintings can be changed and refined through many layers. The artist can begin with a rough sketch of the forms of the painting, and gradually add color and tone. Just as each layer can require time to dry before a new layer can be added, a good paper involves numerous drafts, with breaks in between for the writer to step back and clear his or her head.

So mix your colors carefully, and step up to your easel with confidence. Just make sure you use complementary colors—not complimentary ones!

QUALITY; ALWAYS QUALITY. If a professor asks for a seven-page paper on a specific topic, they would rather get a four-page paper with good, hard facts than a paper filled with fluff. Professors are smart; they can read through your filler language.

—RYAN NAUGHTON
MAPLEWOOD, MINNESOTA
UNIVERSITY OF ST. THOMAS

* * * * * * * *

TAKE THE TOTAL APPROACH. The best papers I wrote were ones I could pull from all different parts of class: the reading, the class discussions, my own notes and insights. The professors are looking for that type of total understanding. That's what an A paper is.

—SARAH DAVID HEYDEMANN
MONTCLAIR, NEW JERSEY

* * * * * * * *

I FIGURED OUT HOW TO WRITE a B+ paper in a jif. I knew the library closed at 11. So, I would show up at 9:30 the night before for a 10-page research paper. I would take out as many books on the topic as possible. Then, I'd go home and find my subject in the index. I'd be able to write a ten-page paper in four to five hours that wove together all these sources so that it seemed really well researched. I called it the B+ method because I always got a minimum of a B+ on the paper.

—RAFAEL
HONG KONG, CHINA
GEORGETOWN UNIVERSITY GPA: 3.4

EVEN WHEN YOU HAVE something intelligent to say, it will only sound stupid if it's not presented well. We write the way we talk, and if we leave out important words when we talk and use slang, that will translate on your paper. I always looked at a grammar book before I wrote a paper.

—TIOMBE EILAND
CHICAGO, ILLINOIS
LOYOLA UNIVERSITY

• • • • • • • •

If you have to write a thesis, don't worry about your thesis statement in the beginning. Just pursue your interests and read, read, read; your topic will develop.

—JASON SIEGEL
BERKELEY, CALIFORNIA
UNIVERSITY OF CALIFORNIA, BERKELEY GPA: 3.85

• • • • • • • •

STRUCTURE YOUR PAPER AROUND an argument and make sure that it is clear, concise, and well organized. My professor used to cross out everything that was extraneous leaving me with four or five sentences on my paper. He'd tell me, this is what you are trying to say.

—J.R.
AUSTIN, TEXAS
UNIVERSITY OF TEXAS, AUSTIN

ONE SUCCESSFUL PROCEDURE

Before I start writing I get all my sources down and type up all the relevant quotes I might use or that might just be good for inspiration later on in the paper. And I write down any and all the questions I have, but I don't answer them until I write the paper. Getting all that down makes it easier. I always have my first sentence start with some kind of contextualization, whether by geography or by era. Introductions are incredibly important for whatever is being said. When you're synthesizing your sources, just make sure to keep referring back to the major point you're trying to make. My dad always told me that doing a paper is like doing geometry: "This therefore this therefore this therefore this." You go through writing a paper the same way you write a proof.

—MAGGIE
NEW YORK, NEW YORK
BROWN UNIVERSITY

THIS IS THE ANSWER!

College papers have to be in active voice, not passive. Most students don't understand this. Here is the easiest tip ever on writing in the active voice.

Write your sentences in this order: Thing doing the action/action being done/receiver of the action. There are all kinds of explanations having to do with grammar terms and so forth, but this is the answer!

Sentences should look like this: The committee is reviewing the bill. *Not:* The bill is being reviewed by the committee. Just think of what's happening, and use this order: the doer, the action, and then the receiver. Easy!

—S.B.
SOUTH BEND, INDIANA
BALL STATE UNIVERSITY

MY BEST FRIEND and I lived in adjoining rooms my sophomore year, and we'd have sessions where we sat down and edited each other's papers. That worked really well for both of us. Even reading someone else's paper on a different subject, I could figure out how to apply her strengths to what I was writing, and incorporate her corrections. It's always good to have someone else read your paper.

—H.D.
WESTIN, CONNECTICUT
SWARTHMORE COLLEGE

• • • • • • • •

IF YOU KEEP UP on your reading and class assignments you will probably retain things and not have to do as much research for your paper. I don't keep up all of the time, so I have to start working on my papers about two to three weeks before they are due in order to do all of the necessary research.

—ANONYMOUS
LOS ANGELES, CALIFORNIA

• • • • • • • •

WRITE WHAT YOU FEEL, write what is on your mind and don't worry about sounding smart. Since English is not my native language, I used to rely on a Thesaurus. Eventually I realized that writing in a simple form always came out much better.

—OMAR FEKEIKI
BERKELEY, CALIFORNIA
ALTURATH UNIVERSITY COLLEGE, BAGHDAD

I could have done a little better in my paper-based classes if I had started my papers earlier and put more effort into them.

—S.P.
DHAKA, BANGLADESH
STANFORD UNIVERSITY

PROFESSORS PREFER QUALITY to quantity. If you ramble too much in a paper because you think it needs to be longer, you will be penalized for it. When my class faces short-answer questions on a quiz, my professor always tells us to make it sweet and short. She tells us to get directly to the point and leave it. And, by adding extra material, you might say something that will make the answer wrong.

—RACHEL ALDRICH
BROOKLYN PARK, MINNESOTA
UNIVERSITY OF WISCONSIN GPA: 3.7

Bring your T.A. an outline; they will go over it with you.

—ANONYMOUS
IRVINE,
CALIFORNIA
UNIVERSITY
OF CALIFORNIA,
SAN DIEGO

PREPARE AN OUTLINE BEFORE you write. I've never gotten below an A on a paper, so I know. The first thing I do is I write a very general, broad outline with a few headings. Then I begin to flesh out each of those headings and the outline becomes more detailed. Then sometimes I start writing out paragraphs that are going to go in each of those sections of the outline. If I were to choose a word to describe this process it would be hierarchical.

—ARTHUR LECHTHOLZ-ZEY
LOS ANGELES, CALIFORNIA
UNIVERISTY OF CALIFORNIA, LOS ANGELES

A STERN MINI-LECTURE ON PLAGIARISM

Referring to outside sources is a good thing. Failing to use proper citations is not. When you present someone else's words or ideas as your own, you are committing plagiarism. This is an attempt to deceive others about your knowledge and/or skill, and it is never acceptable. Professors today have many ways to detect plagiarism. First of all, they read a lot of student work, and they often have a sixth sense that tells them when something doesn't sound authentic. In addition, there are quite a few resources out there for professors who want to investigate a suspicious paper. Keep your conscience clear and your academic record clean—do your own work, and ask for help if you aren't sure of the proper ways to use citations and references.

NO NEED TO SUMMARIZE

One of my duties recently was reading entries for a 1,000-word student essay contest on the book *The Kite Runner* by Khaled Hosseini. I could tell that the book made a strong impression on the entrants. They put in a lot of time and effort, yet many had no chance of winning. Why? They used up a thousand words summarizing the novel, and reached the end of their essay without saying anything new.

I didn't need to read summaries of *The Kite Runner*: I had already read the book three times! And I had no way of knowing whether the students had thought deeply about the themes of the book or related it to their own lives, if they didn't discuss the text rather than merely summarize it. What's more, the contest instructions asked for either a critical analysis of an element of the book, or a personal response: summaries fell into neither category.

In high school, your teachers may have encouraged you to summarize readings in your papers in order to demonstrate your reading comprehension. Now that you're in college, your professors assume that you understand the material, and expect you to interpret and discuss it at a very high level. Your English professor may have taught *Jane Eyre* every semester for the last 30 years. You don't have to tell him that Jane is a governess—but if you discuss the limited career options for women at the time in which the novel is set, and refer to several outside texts, then he'll probably be interested!

IT'S FUNNY HOW SO MANY STUDENTS believe that what they write is divinely inspired and not in need of revision. The better papers are the ones that are revised. Most students procrastinate, which is fine as long as you leave enough time to do three revisions. I've been doing this since high school and I always do well on my papers. I tend to write the paper in the first draft then ten hours later I'll look at it again and change some stuff. Then I leave it for a day and look it over one more time.

—JACK LIGMAN
LANCASTER, CALIFORNIA
UNIVERSITY OF CALIFORNIA, LOS ANGELES

• • • • • • • •

STUDENTS WHO DON'T WRITE well are a lot more successful when they go to their school's writing and/or tutoring center right from the beginning of a writing assignment. The people there help you narrow down your subject, which is usually too broad. They'll point you in the right direction. It may seem embarrassing, but you will get over that right away, and you might as well get on the right track instead of having to go later when you are rushed, which is even more embarrassing.

—S.B.
SOUTH BEND, INDIANA
BALL STATE UNIVERSITY

I WAS WRITING MY FIRST PAPER for Introduction to Humanities. I tried to take everything I heard in the lectures and cram it into one paper. I started to shoot from the hip and throw out as many ideas as I could. I thought it was a great paper. However, I had a million points in the paper, and 999,000 of them were not going to support my thesis. I ended up getting a C-. I spoke to a few writing tutors and one thing they all told me was how important it was to sit down and brainstorm. Construct a solid, coherent argument by writing an outline. When you jump into just writing you tend to stray on tangents and you don't always support your stated thesis.

—ANONYMOUS
LOS ANGELES, CALIFORNIA
STANFORD UNIVERSITY

• • • • • • • •

The best way to write a good paper is to humble yourself. Go to the writing center on campus and get a second set of eyes to read your paper.

—PATRINA LANG
UNIVERSITY PARK, ILLINOIS
SOUTHERN ILLINOIS UNIVERSITY

WHAT KIND OF LEARNER ARE YOU?

Visit these Web sites for quizzes that will help you discover what kind of learner you are. The sites also offer information on matching your study techniques to your learning style.

www.metamath.com/lsweb/dvclearn.htm

www.ncsu.edu/felder-public/ILSdir/styles.htm

www.funderstanding.com/multiple_intelligence.cfm

WHEN I WROTE THESIS-STYLE papers in college, my grade would always be higher when I used examples from the text in every paragraph. It took me a little while to realize this, but once I had it down I started seeing A's instead of B's on my papers. Because a thesis paper is all opinion, I learned that as long as I was supporting my points, I was on target. And once I had the formula down, it became easier to crank out those papers.

—AMANDA TUST
EAST STROUDSBURG, PENNSYLVANIA
UNIVERSITY OF SAN DIEGO

WHY IT'S GOOD TO BE OBVIOUS

Every good paper has a reason for being. We write in order to convince and persuade. If all you are doing is describing a text, historical event, or making a connection that is obvious to everyone, you haven't been digging deep enough.

It's easy to think that good writing must be convoluted and full of big words. In most of your college papers, however, simplicity is best.

Make your professor's life easier and your grade better by observing the following guidelines:

1. State the main idea of your paper right up in the first paragraph. Don't worry about being too obvious—there's no such thing!
2. Keep your paper moving along with strong statements of short to medium length. A sentence needn't be long and complicated to be good.
3. Don't use a big word unless you are 100-percent sure you know what it means. Check the dictionary if you need to. An advisee of mine once wrote about his hopes that one day, all people on earth would co-habit peacefully. He really meant "co-exist": the primary meaning of "co-habit" is that people live together in a sexual relationship without being married. Oops!

I ALWAYS WAITED until the last minute to write my papers: by that I mean I'd start writing three to four days before the due date. I tried writing them earlier, but the words just wouldn't flow. I do my best work when the pressure is on, and that worked for me throughout college.

—Kathryn Lauren La Scala
Niagara Falls, New York
Niagara University

● ● ● ● ● ● ● ●

I USE A PARTICULAR APPROACH to writing papers. Rather than write an outline before I start the paper, I outline as I write. At the beginning of my paper, I write a topic heading. Underneath the heading I write everything I can about that topic. When I'm done, I write a new topic heading that logically follows the first and I repeat the process until I finish my first draft.

—P.
Albany, New York
University of Rochester

● ● ● ● ● ● ● ●

Professors are not stupid. They look beyond your clever writing tricks. They know when you are rambling. I tried to get away with a sloppy paper on "America's Intervention in Third World Countries." I was just rambling about the president and his love for the country of Africa. When I got my paper back, I got a D. And my professor wrote in bold letters, "Africa Is Not a Country, It's A Continent, Jee Whiz."

—Carla Manning
Chicago, Illinois
University of Georgia

BEST PRESENTATIONS EVER

MY PRESENTATION WAS ON THE ILLUSORY nature of the gender binary. It's a complicated, confusing, and often emotionally charged subject, and I knew that in order to get the point across I had to break it down into segments that were easily understood. When I gave the presentation, I wrote symbols on the board (XX, XY) and then started drawing arrows and explaining why XX didn't always lead to XY, and so forth. Using simple symbols helped make the confusing subject matter more concrete and helped the class follow and understand the argument.

—LAURA CARROLL
SALEM, MASSACHUSETTS

• • • • • • • •

I WAS ALREADY GRADUATING, the class was not in my major, and I was doing well in it. I was supposed to take a side in a debate, and I took the politically incorrect side that no one wanted. I completely ad-libbed the whole debate and just made one bold statement after another. People came up to me afterward and said they'd changed their minds about the issue. I just laughed because it wasn't what I really believed at all.

—JESSE MCCREE
SOMERVILLE, MASSACHUSETTS
🏛 BOWDOIN COLLEGE GPA: 3.6

IN MY CAMPAIGNS CLASS, I devised a pitch to raise musical awareness in underprivileged schools. It was a mock presentation to a "school board" and I had an orchestra trio come in and play Mozart to demonstrate the art of sound and the creativity it will spark in kids. My project later lead to a brief internship at a nonprofit orchestra company in my hometown.

—KATHLEEN MCDONALD
TROY, MICHIGAN
MICHIGAN STATE UNIVERSITY

• • • • • • • •

POWERPOINT IS A GOOD WAY to feel like you have some sort of control. You push a button and the next thing happens on the screen. And it takes the spotlight off you.

—MAGGIE
NEW YORK, NEW YORK
BROWN UNIVERSITY

FOUR WAYS TO OVERCOME WRITER'S BLOCK

1. There's nothing more intimidating than a 10-page paper—unless it's a 20-page paper. But how intimidated can you get when all you have to do is fill in one piece of paper? Start with one page of brainstorming. Write down all the ideas that come to your mind, without censoring yourself. Soon you'll be on your way.
2. Still intimidated? Instead of a full page, try an index card. The small size of the card will force you to come up with concise phrases.
3. Ask a friend to sit down with you. As clearly as you can, describe what you want to say in your paper and how you want to say it.
4. Go back to your syllabus or the assignment paper. Rereading your professor's instructions may give you some ideas.

You're Up: Studying For & Taking Exams

I've always been good at school and not so good at sports, so I remember big tests the way athletes remember big games. I can picture myself back in college, wearing my lucky green sweatshirt, opening a blue book, and writing my college's honor pledge: "no aid, no violation." The hum of the fluorescent lights in the hushed lecture hall was, for me, like the roar of the crowd in a stadium. Full of adrenaline, I leaped into (mental) action. More recently, I took a graduate school exam where the professor allowed us to refer to our class readings and notes. My papers filled a small rolling suitcase. I arrived extra early at the test room and arranged my papers in stacks, divided by topic, along the wall behind my chair. Those stacks were my teammates, coaches, and cheerleaders, and they helped me to victory—I got an A on the exam and in the class.

Short answer, multiple-choice, essay—whatever form your test questions take, what matters is whether you've learned the course material and become skilled at expressing your knowledge while the clock is ticking.

Lots of the student tips in this chapter reflect the importance of active learning. Creating your own (instructor-permitted) cheat sheet, identifying core concepts, teaching a study buddy—any method that gets you thinking, and not just memorizing, is good.

Once you've got the learning down, you can refine your test-taking moves; everything from starting with the easy questions to making quick outlines before embarking on essays. Soon you'll be a champion, even if the real cheers don't start until you're back at home and receive your grades after the semester ends.

I ONCE PREPARED FOR AN OPEN-BOOK and open-note exam in physics. You were allowed to bring in a double-sided crib sheet. But, I guess I blew off the class when the professor said which book the test would come from. So, I prepared my crib sheet from the wrong book. When I went into the test, I had the wrong book and a crib sheet with none of the applicable formulas. Basically, I never had a chance. I think I'm a cautionary tale. If you're going to blow off a class, make sure to check in with one of your classmates and if it's an open book test, for God's sake make sure to use the right book.

—M.J.
New York, New York
Washington University in St. Louis GPA: 2.16

• • • • • • • •

I LIST FACTS FOR THE VARIOUS TOPICS covered on the test. These are the things I memorize. As soon as I get the test, I briefly look at the questions, and in the margins I write a few facts for each one. Then I write out each answer. I try not to BS, because it is very obvious to the teachers when students do that. I also leave the last sentence open-ended, rather than making some final statement, so that if I think of other facts later I can add them on.

—S.B.
South Bend, Indiana
Ball State University

DO NOT DENY YOURSELF anything the week before exams. I mean, don't stress out about spending the extra five dollars on a smoothie or iced latte. There's so much stress before finals, and this is one really easy piece to remove.

—TIM
SANTA CRUZ, CALIFORNIA
SONOMA STATE UNIVERSITY

• • • • • • • •

For multiple-choice exams I usually focus on definitions, but for essays I focus on key concepts and examples. Also, get some sleep and don't spend the whole night studying!

—JODIE PIETRUCHA
MISHAWAKA, INDIANA
INDIANA UNIVERSITY, SOUTH BEND

• • • • • • • •

FOR AMERICAN HISTORY, I always took notes divided by year and category. Before a big quiz, I would rewrite all of my notes and read them aloud. It really cemented the information in my mind.

—ETHAN
MILFORD, CONNECTICUT
SOUTHERN CONNECTICUT STATE UNIVERSITY

SOB STORIES

I WENT TO GREAT LENGTHS to make flash cards to help me study for my art history final exam. I made color photocopies of pages and pages of artwork and added extensive notes about each artist, and even color-coded them to correspond with different art periods and styles. The night before the test, I started to fall asleep as I was studying my beautiful flash cards in the library. I decided to leave and finish studying at home. When I got home I realized I had left my cards back at the library, which was now closed! I stayed up and studied all night and ended up doing well on the test. When I went back to the library the next morning to retrieve my notes, they were nowhere to be found. You can probably sense that I am still a bit broken up about it!

—STEVE
SOUTH ORANGE, NEW JERSEY
UNIVERSITY OF CALIFORNIA, RIVERSIDE GPA: 3.5

• • • • • • • •

I ONCE SLEPT THROUGH AN EXAM because my alarm clock didn't go off. I was a freshman and I freaked out. I went to get a dean's note. I thought the dean would understand that I was a good, conscientious student, but he went nuts on me and I started crying. He did give me the note. I think he felt bad; he was really nice to me every time he saw me after that.

—JESSICA
LOS ANGELES, CALIFORNIA

THE WORST MISTAKE YOU CAN MAKE is studying from someone else's cheat sheet instead of just making your own. I tried it my first semester here and I just didn't learn anything at all. My friend got an A, and I got a B, even though we studied the exact same thing. I learned that by designing your own study sheet, you actually learn more than just memorizing what someone gives you.

—S.A.
FRAMINGHAM, MASSACHUSETTS
UNIVERSITY OF SOUTHERN CALIFORNIA GPA: 3.6

Read the directions before you take any test. It seems simple enough, but you never know.

—GAVIN BODKIN BRADFORD, NEW HAMPSHIRE WESLEYAN UNIVERSITY

* * * * * * * *

SOME STUDENTS THINK they need to memorize the class material to do well on an exam, but I take another approach: I do everything I can to understand the core concept of the subject. When I study for an important exam, I think about four or five themes we talked about during class and write down everything I know about them. Then I go outside of my class materials and read what I can online and in the library to get a broader understanding. I've found that most essays don't ask you to repeat everything you know about a subject: they ask you to critically analyze something. The only way to do that is to have a good, well-rounded understanding of the subject.

—JASON PAUL TORREANO
LOCKPORT, NEW YORK
STATE UNIVERSITY OF NEW YORK, BROCKPORT

THERE ARE THREE THINGS you need to do to get an A on an exam. Study the homework assignments, study the reading and class notes on your own, then get together with a small group and go over everything. There are times when I haven't done all three and my test scores reflected it.

—COURTLAND
BERKELEY, CALIFORNIA
UNIVERSITY OF CALIFORNIA, BERKELEY GPA: 3.6

• • • • • • • •

ONE OF THE MOST USEFUL THINGS I do to prepare for exams is to study with friends from my classes. The libraries at my university have study spaces with white boards. We find a study space and quiz each other with flash cards that we've prepared ahead of time, and we help each other understand complicated subject matter. We use the white board to draw chemical structures and chemical reactions that we need to know for the exam.

—VANESSA HOFFMAN
WASHINGTON, D.C.
CORNELL UNIVERSITY

• • • • • • • •

TREAT AN ESSAY EXAM like you would a mini-thesis. The best bet is to sit down at the beginning of the test and do an outline as if you are writing a paper. Have a concrete format so you don't stray off in the limited time and space that you have.

—ANONYMOUS
LOS ANGELES, CALIFORNIA
STANFORD UNIVERSITY

WORST STUDY MISTAKE

THINKING THAT JUST BECAUSE we did not cover textbook information in class it wouldn't be on the exam was worth a huge portion of my grade. It's always best to ask what will be on the exam; we all know that assuming simply makes an ass of you.

—JULIA JAWORSKI
BLOOMFIELD HILLS, MICHIGAN
MICHIGAN STATE UNIVERSITY GPA: 3.83

• • • • • • • •

I FORGOT THERE WAS A BACK to my study guide. Therefore there was an entire page of 30 terms that I didn't study. Take the extra two seconds to flip it over; you'll thank yourself later.

—KATHLEEN MCDONALD
TROY, MICHIGAN
MICHIGAN STATE UNIVERSITY

• • • • • • • •

DON'T SEE SALVATION IN SOMEONE just because she's cute. I was struggling through a poetry class and I asked this girl if she wanted to study together. I figured she could only help me. But, she barely knew anything herself, I wound up getting a D+ on the test, and she wound up dropping out.

—M.J.
HOBOKEN, NEW JERSEY
UNIVERSITY OF PENNSYLVANIA

I FIRST CHECK THE LECTURE NOTES and make new notes. Then I go home and read the book for the details and to expand on the notes I took in class. When it comes time for exams, I have my own cheat sheet that covers everything. I still have to study like crazy for the tests, but I do feel prepared going into them.

—Cao Hong
Walnut, California
University of California, Los Angeles GPA: 3.95

* * * * * * * *

IF I DON'T KNOW THE ANSWER on a multiple choice question, I try to look for one answer that is unique in some way from all the others; that is usually the right one. Or, I knock off ones that I know can't be true and guess from the ones I have left. Sometimes it helps to leave it blank and go back, because the rest of the questions might give clues to the answer you're looking for.

—A.S.
Chicago, Illinois
University of Wisconsin

* * * * * * * *

I HAD TO MEMORIZE a map for a geography class. So, I made two copies, one with the names in place, and another with the names whited out. I looked at both for a couple of minutes every night before going to bed, and I ended up doing really well on the test.

—Maryse Shaina Pearce
Cambria Heights, New York
Washington University in St Louis GPA: 3.4

WHEN I WENT TO GRADUATE SCHOOL for elementary education, I faced three huge tests, and passing them was necessary to become certified. The tests were a big deal. It took me three or more hours to answer the 100 multiple-choice questions and write a long essay at the end. To make sure I was in top shape for them, I always went to bed early the night before and ate a good breakfast of cereal, a banana and orange juice that morning. I didn't want to be worrying about my growling stomach halfway through the test.

—KATHRYN LAUREN LA SCALA
NIAGARA FALLS, NEW YORK
NIAGARA UNIVERSITY

• • • • • • • • •

I'LL TELL YOU WHEN *not* to study:
1) When your girlfriend's over. Study dates quickly morph into real dates. This is especially true on the night before the exam. Conjugate Spanish verbs before you consummate your college flings.
2) The night before you're scheduled to work at your internship. Odds are good that the internship is more valuable in terms of your future career than your education. Don't disappoint your boss because you just had to go through your psych notes one more time.

—SAM WEAVER
MINNEAPOLIS, MINNESOTA
MARQUETTE UNIVERSITY

CELEBRATING AFTER A TEST

IF I DO WELL ON AN EXAM I'll go out and celebrate. Once, after a midterm freshman year, my friends and I went fountain-hopping here. Stanford is famous for its fountains, so we went all around campus and swam around in every fountain, tossed each other in, and just had fun.

—JERRY LEE
SAN DIEGO, CALIFORNIA
STANFORD UNIVERSITY

. . . .

I LIVED IN A MAMMOTH DUPLEX with seven of my close friends, and the afternoon we all finished our tests, we congregated on the roof with two coolers of beer and a stereo blaring "We Are the Champions." After a while, we collected a large mass of beer cans and decided that the best way to get rid of the beer cans was to hit them off the roof with an old golf club that someone had found lying around. Then a cop rolled by and demanded that we stop hitting golf balls off our roof. We politely informed him that we were hitting beer cans and not golf balls, and he responded, "Oh, well, okay, just don't break anything." Finals can be really stressful, and the only way to alleviate that stress is to do the stupidest thing you can think of, once they are finished.

—ZACHARY URNESS
POLSON, MONTANA
UNIVERSITY OF ST. THOMAS

GROUP THERAPY

COLLEGE IS COMPETITIVE, but that doesn't mean you have to work alone all the time. Working with classmates can be extremely helpful, especially if you have multiple deadlines. Be willing to share your thoughts and insights with others, and be open to receive theirs in return.

—JACOB SZE
ELLENVILLE, NEW YORK
CORNELL UNIVERSITY

• • • • • • • •

STUDY GROUPS ARE BENEFICIAL for two reasons. First you get to share your own knowledge with others and that helps you learn. The second reason is that you benefit from someone else's knowledge of something you may not understand. If you know something yourself, you get an opportunity to teach it to someone else in the group which in itself is a great way to study because it solidifies that knowledge in your mind. When you know you can teach something to someone you can say, "I've now mastered that subject." Just remember not to ever go into a group without knowing anything because no one will want to work with you.

—TREVOR EDMONDS
BERKELEY, CALIFORNIA
UNIVERSITY OF CALIFORNIA, BERKELEY GPA: 3.5

STUDYING IN A GROUP IS EXCELLENT when preparing for multiple-choice exams. Study with a group by quizzing each other with possible answers, because that's how the format of the exam will be. Group studying for exams like essays is not helpful, because they require your own synthesis of the information.

—A.S.
CHICAGO, ILLINOIS
UNIVERSITY OF WISCONSIN

• • • • • • • •

DON'T STUDY FOR FINALS WITH A GROUP of friends who are all studying different things. Our whole concept behind the idea was to motivate each other to continue to study. Instead, we each got about 15 minutes of good quality studying. We kept getting off-task, talking about the latest gossip. The four-girl study group turned into a 10-person get-together in the library. I was not prepared for my final the next day. I couldn't remember any of the definitions, but I could remember all the gossip the night before!

—LESLEY
ORLAND PARK, ILLINOIS
BALL STATE UNIVERSITY

I WAS IN A STUDY GROUP ONCE with a bunch of friends. We had so much fun talking about movies and sports that we didn't realize we only had a few minutes before class started and had accomplished nothing.

—MATT BOWEN
BALTIMORE, MARYLAND
UNIVERSITY OF MARYLAND

• • • • • • • • •

MY STUDY GROUPS WERE MAINLY people in my major. It was informal. We'd meet at the lounge in the department's building. Everyone would ask questions and someone would explain. Others might have a better grasp of the concepts of the course. We'd share ideas.

—ELIZABETH ANNE ALARIO
WARREN, NEW JERSEY
RUTGERS UNIVERSITY

• • • • • • • • •

IF YOU ARE GOING TO BE A PART of a study group, make sure it's not with your girlfriend. My girlfriend and I tried to study together, but we spent all night studying each other instead of biology. After we saw our grades we found new groups.

—TODD LUCAS
CHICAGO, ILLINOIS
SOUTHERN ILLINOIS UNIVERSITY

STUDY GROUPS ARE REALLY HELPFUL if you get the right people. I took a media criticism class where the assignment was to watch and critique a film. I chose American Beauty. First, in order to find the themes and symbolism, it was necessary to watch the film over and over, which is more fun when you are in a group. Second, everyone had many different ideas and interpretations, which was really helpful. Without the group, my ideas would have been cut by half.

—LIZ A. POPE
AUBURN, CALIFORNIA
SONOMA STATE UNIVERSITY

• • • • • • • •

DON'T STUDY WITH PEOPLE OUT OF SYMPATHY. I was carrying an A- going into my calculus final. These two girls I knew were both hopelessly lost, so I decided to help them. I figured it was a nice thing to do and it would help me solidify the material in my own mind. But, they were so hopelessly confused that I didn't get any studying done and they just ended up confusing me. I wound up getting a D on the final and wrecking my grade for the course.

—M.J.
HOBOKEN, NEW JERSEY
UNIVERSITY OF PENNSYLVANIA

FOR EVERY CHAPTER that will be covered on the exam, start studying that many days ahead. I would do a chapter a day, and also review the chapter I'd done the day before.

—ERICA
SYRACUSE, NEW YORK
SYRACUSE UNIVERSITY

• • • • • • • •

I always bring bananas and granola bars into my exams. Both snacks are healthy and not messy. I can eat them quietly and not disturb other people.

—ANONYMOUS
NEW YORK, NEW YORK
STANFORD UNIVERSITY GPA: 3.7

• • • • • • • •

THE CHEAT SHEET IS YOUR FRIEND. Don't bring this into the exam—I've seen college careers ruined by this, and your professor will realize your dishonesty no matter how deft you are at concealing your hidden advantage. However, the formation of this guide will help you retain the knowledge you're studying.

—SAM WEAVER
MINNEAPOLIS, MINNESOTA
MARQUETTE UNIVERSITY

THREE TEST-TAKING TIPS THAT SOUND SILLY BUT WORK WONDERFULLY

1. If you have friends in the same class, tell them that even though you love them, you don't want them to talk to you right before the test. You don't want to psych each other out by talking about how nervous you are.
2. If your test is being given in a different room than where you normally have class, take a personal field trip to the test location. Sit in one of the seats for a few minutes. Look around the room. Is it warm? Chilly? Now you know how to dress on test day. You also know how to get there, so you won't get lost on the big day and arrive for the test feeling panicky.
3. Pick one outfit and wear it whenever you study for the test. Wear the same outfit when you take the test. Honestly, this will help you remember what you studied! (But it's okay to wash the outfit before test day.)

TIPS ON PREPARING LABS

READ YOUR MANUAL, and do what your TAs tell you to do. But before you do all of that, make sure to do your pre-lab. In pre-lab you test your theory. That means you write about it and predict the results you expect to get. If you didn't do a pre-lab you would walk into the lab and have no idea what's going on. If you don't know what's going on in the lab, the people around you will get annoyed. They will ask you things like, "Did you read the lab manual ... why didn't you read it?"

—ANONYMOUS
HOLMDEL, NEW JERSEY
CALIFORNIA INSTITUTE OF TECHNOLOGY

• • • • • • • • •

THE LAB MANUAL GIVES YOU the bare bones on what you need to know to get through the lab, but in my opinion, understanding the physics behind the lab, which you can do by reading other books (some that are not on the syllabus), makes it much simpler. A lot of the Dover books, which are paperback reprints of the best physics and math books around, are usually pretty easy to understand.

—B.R.
LONG BEACH, CALIFORNIA
CARNEGIE MELLON UNIVERSITY

GETTING A GOOD TA IN LAB is the key to passing. A good TA is someone you can ask, "What does the switch on this thing do?" A good TA will answer, "This switch controls this." A bad TA will answer, "What do you think this switch does?" If you make one mistake, it might mess up your entire lab, but a good TA will take off for the first mistake and tell you to correct it next time, while a bad TA will take off every time it shows up in your lab, even though it's the same mistake, which isn't fair and can destroy your grade.

—MARISSA CEVALLOS
CHARLESTON, WEST VIRGINIA
CALIFORNIA INSTITUTE OF TECHNOLOGY

• • • • • • • • •

I READ THE LAB MANUAL so I can understand the theory behind what I will be doing in lab that day. I'll map out my strategy so I know what supplies I'll be using, when I'll be using them, and where. I've gone into lab unprepared and I don't like it. I felt totally ignorant and felt as if I just looked unprepared; as if everyone was looking at me. I knew that if I had prepared, I would have known what was going on. There are lab partners to help you out, but I don't like depending on them.

—KRISTIN
INGLEWOOD, CALIFORNIA
UNIVERSITY OF CALIFORNIA, LOS ANGELES

IT WAS MY VERY FIRST FINAL as a freshman, and I woke up just five minutes before class. I had slept through my alarm and my roommates had left me. I knew I just had to get there so I threw on some shoes and ran to my final in my pajamas. I got there right before my prof locked the door ... and still got an A!

—BRIDGET SCRABECK
LAKEVILLE, MINNESOTA
UNIVERSITY OF ST. THOMAS

. . . .

OUR TESTS FOCUS ON PROBLEM SOLVING, not memorization. The problem sets that we do each week are a big part of our grade. They take a lot of time and we usually try to collaborate in groups to get them done. It's really funny; we have three problems on each set and each one takes us hours just to understand it. But once you get through your homework, you are essentially prepared for the tests here.

—LEYAN LO
BASKING RIDGE, NEW JERSEY
CALIFORNIA INSTITUTE OF TECHNOLOGY GPA: 3.7

. . . .

IN PRE-MED YOU SHOULD START studying for tests about a week ahead. Sometimes I'll even skip a couple of days of lecture classes—not my smaller classes—to devote my full attention to studying for a big test.

—J.W.
ST. LOUIS, MISSOURI
WASHINGTON UNIVERSITY IN ST. LOUIS GPA: 4

> *I would repeat definitions and sentences to myself out loud. I even went back to elementary school, and wrote words down five times each.*
>
> —KARINNE SPENCER
> CHICAGO, ILLINOIS
> SOUTHERN ILLINOIS UNIVERSITY

SPECIAL ACCOMMODATIONS

You may be too young to have watched *Beverly Hills 90210* when it was first broadcast, but maybe you have caught some reruns. Remember the episode when Donna Martin thinks she is incapable of taking tests? Fortunately, her principal sends Donna to a learning difference specialist, and in the end Donna is approved for special testing accommodations. Isn't it nice how big life problems can be solved all within one hour-long episode?

In real life, the process of getting academic accommodations takes a little bit longer, but it happens all the time. Many students have a physical or learning condition and need special accommodations so that they can perform to the best of their ability. Some students need to take their exams in a quiet room with no distractions. Other students need extra time on assignments. Some students need a scribe to take class notes for them. Others need a physical accommodation such as being permitted to type their exams instead of writing them by hand.

If you feel that accommodations might be appropriate for you, you can start by talking to your advisor or by looking in your college directory for an ADA Coordinator. ADA stands for Americans with Disabilities Act, the law that says, basically, that having a disability should not be a barrier to getting an education.

FOUR WAYS TO COPE WITH TEST ANXIETY

Your college probably offers workshops on coping with test anxiety, and I encourage you to attend one. For now, here are four quick tips:

1. Breathe! This is the simplest thing you can do to help yourself calm down.
2. Try to avoid cramming right up until the last minute. Instead, relax and go to bed early. This will reduce your test anxiety.
3. Do the easy questions first to build up your confidence.
4. What do you do if you panic in the middle of the test and your mind goes blank? Believe it or not, this happens to lots of people. Remember that the panic you are experiencing is a physical reaction to a stressful situation, and does not necessarily mean that you don't know enough of the answers to do well. Give yourself a moment to travel in your mind to a place where you can feel relaxed and safe. Then gently return to your exam, knowing that you will get through this experience.

Brainbusting:
On Cramming
& All-Nighters

In this chapter, you'll hear about the lengths students go to when they get down to the wire preparing for an exam or writing a paper. There are some desperate situations described here! But something is missing. What you won't hear about in this chapter is a path many students have taken when they ran out of time: the path of cheating and plagiarism.

Of course, some people decide to cheat or plagiarize early on, but in my experience most breaches of academic integrity occur when students find they've painted themselves into a corner and can't see any other way out. Maybe they are too rushed, tired, or stressed to check over their paper carefully enough, and they plagiarize by accident. Or maybe they buy a paper on the Internet, or bring forbidden materials into the test room, deciding to risk possible detection instead of taking a definite low grade.

I've heard these students' stories while sitting on conduct committees and I have a lot of sympathy for them. I can understand the temptation to cheat when you're overwhelmed with work and time is running out. The fact that the students' actions were understandable, however, didn't mean the conduct committee could condone them.

You already have plenty of reasons to manage your time and organize your work so that it's spread out over the semester. You know better than to leave everything until the last minute. But just in case you need one more motivating factor, use this one: Avoid temptation—don't place yourself in that difficult position where cheating seems to be the best way out.

THE ALL-NIGHTER PARTIES to study usually turn into major distractions. You're supposed to be studying for your theology midterm; instead, you decide to go find a pumpkin to drop from your sixth-story dorm window in hopes of putting off your homework for one more hour.

—LAURA GLASS
GOLDEN VALLEY, MINNESOTA
UNIVERSITY OF ST. THOMAS

* * * * * * * *

I'M FROM EASTERN EUROPE, so coffee is my life. I normally have at least two cups of coffee a day (espresso, strong). All-nighters would include at least two of those, after seven Cokes, and sometimes Red Bull or some other energy drink.

—LILIA
SOFIA, BULGARIA
GEORGETOWN UNIVERSITY GPA: 2.4

* * * * * * * *

IN FRENCH CLASS we are given this workbook that we are supposed to keep up during the course; however, since the professor never checks it until the end of the quarter, I left it for the last minute. I had to stay up all night before my last French class to complete an entire quarter of homework. By the end of the night, I was speaking French to people accidentally: someone would ask me a question and I would answer him in the wrong language.

—NATHANIEL
PHILADELPHIA, PENNSYLVANIA
STANFORD UNIVERSITY GPA: 3.7

Studying can easily make me fall asleep, but the sound of maniacal typing keeps me up.

—TIFFANY LOPES
NEWARK, NEW JERSEY
PENNSYLVANIA STATE UNIVERSITY

EVEN THOUGH I TRY to avoid all-nighters, I've actually felt really good the next day, like I'm running on some kind of magic adrenaline. I feel invigorated for the first 12 hours. Then it hits me and I'm dead for that entire evening.

—ANONYMOUS
NEW YORK, NEW YORK
STANFORD UNIVERSITY GPA: 3.7

• • • • • • • •

My three friends and I made it through a night of studying by setting the goal of going to IHOP at 7 a.m. That helped us to stay focused.

—NATALIE JARECKI
BOCA RATON, FLORIDA
WASHINGTON UNIVERSITY GPA: 3.42

• • • • • • • •

MY JUNIOR YEAR, when I was cramming for an organic chemistry exam, I chugged a gigantic Dunkin' Donuts coffee and then took some No Doz in order to keep myself awake. It backfired: I was so hyper I had to run a couple of laps through the dorms just to calm down. I completely blew my prime study hours.

—M.J.
HOBOKEN, NEW JERSEY
UNIVERSITY OF PENNSYLVANIA

It was my last exam, and I was leaving on a plane two hours after it finished. My room was completely bare, except for my computer. My friend came over and we studied the entire night. It was the first time I'd stayed up all night for an exam. By the time dawn rolled around we were glassy-eyed, but prepared. It wasn't the smartest idea I've ever had, but I did make an A. If you're going to deprive yourself of sleep, you might as well get something out of it!

—Amanda Nelson-Duac
Granbury, Texas
George Washington University GPA: 3.6

• • • • • • • •

I stayed up for almost 48 hours studying for a test and was so tired the next morning that I ended up falling down the stairs from my loft. Don't procrastinate that badly. All-nighters should be for reviewing the information, not for trying to learn it all in one night. Take breaks or you will go crazy, and it's always helpful to share those kinds of nights with a friend who won't distract you too badly. It's nice to share the misery of lack of sleep with someone.

—A.C.C.
Austin, Texas
University of Texas at Austin GPA: 3.8

A GREAT AWAKENING?

Just walk around your campus in the morning and count the giant cups clutched by sleepy-looking students in sweat pants. A casual first date is often a "coffee date." Pick out a brown sweater in a catalog and the description will probably call it "mocha" or "espresso." You can probably name at least one computing technology with a coffee-related name. Caffeine, of course, is found in a variety of beverages and foods, although we associate it most often with coffee.

Note that in this chapter, just as in the others, you get a wide range of opinions on this popular legal drug. Lilia from Bulgaria says that coffee is her life. A.F. from Cincinnati laments that too much caffeine makes you feel "sluggish and gross the next day."

The bottom line is, too much caffeine is bad for your body and your wallet (think about it: Two or three expensive coffee drinks a day, at around five dollars each, adds up to a truly enormous sum at the end of the semester. Even a couple of cheap deli coffees every day can put a real dent in your budget.) My advice to you on this matter comes from *Justine*, a novel by Lawrence Durrell that I was obsessed with in college: "Indulge but refine."

I'VE NEVER HAD TO PULL an all-nighter, although I've been close. My craziest experience was during my freshman year, finishing up a paper by the midnight submit deadline, then scrambling to finish another paper by 8:00 that morning. I slept for about five hours and barely turned in the paper on time.

—ANONYMOUS
NEW YORK, NEW YORK
🏛 TULANE UNIVERSITY

• • • • • • • •

I DIDN'T SLEEP ONCE for three days in a row. I was up for seventy-five hours; my roommate counted. It was last quarter, which is when all of the activities are taking place and where I took all of my hardest classes. I'm in a music group and we were preparing for our spring show, and at the same time I had all of these projects to send in and I needed to get the work done, so I was up forever. I will never do that again.

—NANA KOFI KORANTENG OHENE-ADU
ACCRA, GHANA
🏛 STANFORD UNIVERSITY

• • • • • • • •

POWER NAPS ARE KEY, for all-nighters and for life. The naps have to be short; you cannot let your brain get into the deep-sleep mode because then you will feel exhausted rather than rested and revived.

—NICOLE SPENCE
ATLANTA, GEORGIA
🏛 EMORY UNIVERSITY GPA: 3.71

REALLY CRAZY ALL-NIGHTERS

I ONCE SLEPT THROUGH a history exam after staying up all night studying for it. I made flash cards, I memorized everything, I practiced writing my essays, and at around six in the morning I closed my eyes for a second. The next thing I knew, it was ten; my exam was at eight. I tried to get my professor to let me make it up, but he would not budge.

—ANONYMOUS
EAST BRUNSWICK, NEW JERSEY
GEORGE WASHINGTON UNIVERSITY

• • • • • • • • •

I HAD A SIX-PAGE ASTRONOMY PAPER due the morning after the midnight opening of one of the Harry Potter movies. A bunch of friends were going and I knew I'd be disappointed if I didn't go. I didn't start my paper until that afternoon, and by showtime, I only had three pages. I knew it was a bad idea, but I went to the movie anyway, had a good time, got back at 3:30 a.m. and had to write the rest of the paper. I finished around 6 a.m., just as the sun was coming up. Somehow I pulled off an A-, but I felt like total crap the next day.

—ALEX WALL
EASTON, PENNSYLVANIA

I WAS UP ALL NIGHT TRYING TO FINISH a music theory paper, but I kept dozing off. So I did what I never thought I'd do: I took No Doz to help me stay awake. The pill made me paranoid: I was walking around campus constantly scratching my body, thinking something was crawling on me; I kept looking over my shoulder, thinking somebody was about to attack me. It took a whole day for full recovery.

—CHANA SERGEANT
CHICAGO, ILLINOIS
NORTHERN ILLINOIS UNIVERSITY

MY THIRD TERM IN COLLEGE, I had some really hard classes and had to pull all-nighters to study for my finals. I don't know how many nights in a row I stayed up because it started to get a little blurry. I think I took three- or four-hour naps every day, or every other day, for about a week. I don't think I could have done anything differently because my classes were so hard. In the end I did really well, so it was worth it.

—DANIEL
MARLTON, NEW JERSEY
CALIFORNIA INSTITUTE OF TECHNOLOGY

I STAYED UP ONE TOO MANY NIGHTS writing papers. I had three papers due in two days, followed by an exam. I was so tired and confused that I lost track of time. I went out to celebrate after I turned in my last paper, but when I got back to my dorm around midnight, my friends asked me why I wasn't studying. They reminded me that I had a test the next day. I'd thought I had a whole day and night to prepare; I'd lost a whole day.

—JULIE
BEVERLY HILLS, CALIFORNIA
UNIVERSITY OF SOUTHERN CALIFORNIA GPA: 3.4

• • • • • • • • •

I SIGNED UP FOR A PLAYWRITING CLASS while juggling the biggest load I'd ever taken: 21 credits. I put off writing my script until two days before it was due. Then, I went on a binge of Coca-Colas and—don't try this at home, kids—Adderall. I stayed up for two consecutive nights and days, skipping all my classes, writing the entire time. I finished the play—but unfortunately what I'd begun as a comedy slowly disintegrated into a kind of sleep-deprived hallucination.

—LAUREN
ST. LOUIS, MISSOURI
WASHINGTON UNIVERSITY IN ST. LOUIS GPA: 3.8

IF I DO NOT GET AT LEAST nine hours of sleep I do not function very well. I will cram for a couple of hours before bed, then, for an hour before I go to sleep, do something to relax. Then I wake up in the morning and review. I find that sleeping helps more than staying up all night trying to memorize things.

—ADELAIDE WEAVER
WOODBURY, MINNESOTA
🏛 UNIVERSITY OF MINNESOTA

• • • • • • • •

BECAUSE I WAS SO INVOLVED in student media—the newspaper, two different magazines, and once in a while, the TV station—I spent most of my time studying in a way that wasn't like studying: If you get involved in student activities related to your major, you'll be studying without even realizing that you're studying, and that's the stuff that will stay with you.

—JACLYN YOUHANA
LIBERTY TOWNSHIP, OHIO

• • • • • • • •

IF I PLAN ON STUDYING ALL NIGHT, and I try not to do this too often, I *never* do it with other people. Either there is 1) too much conversation, 2) too much whining, or 3) too much bad influence, as in, "I'm too tired to stay up. Are you really going to stay up? I'm just going to lie down for a minute … " I say, do it alone!

—J.B.
JACKSON, MICHIGAN
🏛 UNIVERSITY OF MICHIGAN GPA: 3.5

I HAD TO STAY UP AND WRITE a 10-page paper once because I decided to put it off until the day it was due. Since my roommate was asleep, I had to build a tent around my desk so he couldn't see the light. I finished the paper and fell asleep in class the next morning. Only do an all-nighter when you need to write a five-page paper.

—JOE
NEW MILFORD, CONNECTICUT
UNIVERSITY OF CONNECTICUT GPA: 3

• • • • • • • • •

I KNOW EVERYBODY WAITS till the last minute, but try to start things earlier than the day or night before they're due. Even if you just outline your paper and figure out what you're going to say before that final push, it will make the writing process easier.

—ALEX WALL
EASTON, PENNSYLVANIA

• • • • • • • • •

I PROCRASTINATE A LOT, so I would have to read everything the night before the exam to try to digest it all. It actually worked for me because I have a good short-term memory. It didn't work in terms of retaining the material (I couldn't tell you anything about it once school ended), but the cramming helped me whip through an exam and do well on it.

—VERONICA
TORONTO, CANADA
CASE WESTERN RESERVE UNIVERSITY

Whenever I stay up past 3 a.m. to study I get crazy, talking weird and making weird noises. I get so exhausted trying to keep myself up, it just isn't worth it.

—LAUREN
HAWTHORNE,
CALIFORNIA
STANFORD
UNIVERSITY
GPA: 3.5

LESSON LEARNED

I once started a final research paper at 11 p.m. I drank Red Bull all night and stayed up until 9 a.m. I must have been delirious, because I had my roommate (who was failing out of college at the time) proof my paper while I fell asleep on a couch. I was 10 minutes late for my class and totally nauseous the whole time. I barely got a C. I pull all-nighters now, but it's different. I don't stay up until 8 a.m. I get the paper or project done in four hours. I break up writing in different parts rather than one long chunk. I have at least three different people proofread my paper: usually, it's my dad, my sister, and someone in my class whom I know well and who does well.

—MICHAEL ABRAMOVITZ
ALTA LOMA, CALIFORNIA
UNIVERSITY OF ARIZONA GPA: 2.65

IT MAY BE TEMPTING to pump yourself full of caffeine and sugar all through those endless nights of studying, but it doesn't work well, and you just end up feeling sluggish and gross the next day. What does work is getting that caffeine in before 10 p.m. and then drinking water for the rest of your study night. I was much more effective later at night, and my body thanked me for it the next day.

—A.F.
CINCINNATI, OHIO
MARQUETTE UNIVERSITY GPA: 3.5

I'VE TRIED TO PULL ALL-NIGHTERS, but I always fall asleep. I was up one night studying at about four in the morning; at that point I decided that I wouldn't be productive anymore, so I went to sleep.

—SHARAREH SADAGHIANI
SAN JOSE, CALIFORNIA
STANFORD UNIVERSITY

* * * * * * * *

I didn't sleep for three days and ate nothing when I was finishing my senior thesis. But, I handed it in on time and got a pretty good grade.

—JONATHAN
BROOKLYN, NEW YORK

* * * * * * * *

I ONCE HAD A PAPER to write and an exam to study for; I left both until the last night. By the time I was done studying for the test, it was 2 a.m. and I still had to write the paper, which I hadn't even researched yet. At that point, even Coca-Cola doesn't work. So, I started playing Blind Melon's song "No Rain" for hours until I was done with the paper. I probably played it 60 or 70 times.

—RAFAEL
HONG KONG, CHINA
GEORGETOWN UNIVERSITY GPA: 3.4

WRITING MY FINAL SEMINAR paper about the use of underworld imagery in modern poetry, sitting in the kitchen nursing my fourth cup of magic all-nighter brew (equal parts coffee and hot chocolate, plus sugar), I was jerked out of my computer daze at 2 a.m. by three of my housemates running in and screaming, "Distraction monkeys!" After declaring a universal snack break and tap dancing around the kitchen amidst our hysterical laughter, we were all much more awake and much less stressed out than we had been. Then we all went back to our respective papers and kept writing and drinking caffeine until dawn.

—LAURA CARROLL
SALEM, MASSACHUSETTS

I LIVED OFF CAMPUS in an apartment with four other girls. For some reason we were big fans of doing our work together, even though it was different work. During finals week of our senior year, we decided we'd all wait until the last minute to study. This resulted in a week of four of us crammed into my room with our laptops and piles of junk food. We stayed up until all hours of the night that week; working, talking and eating. Each morning we'd find ourselves with terrible sugar crashes and empty brains.

—LISA FREEDMAN
NEW YORK, NEW YORK

I HAD A TERM PROJECT DUE in my research methods class, one of those 20-page papers applying everything that has been taught in class. Throughout the term we had done assignments that were to be used in this term paper, so I had the components of the paper; I just needed to put it together and add to it. Did I mention that this paper was worth roughly 50 percent of my final grade? I naturally put this assignment off until the last minute. I started working on it the day before it was due, stayed up all night working feverishly on it, stopping only for short snack breaks. I finished the paper around 6 a.m. the morning it was due. When I returned to class a week later I received my graded term paper, an A, with a note beside it saying it was the highest score in the class. If that teacher had only known about my all-nighter.

—J.B.
RIVERSIDE, CALIFORNIA
CALIFORNIA STATE UNIVERSITY, SAN BERNARDINO

· · · · · · · · ·

I ONLY PULLED ONE ALL-NIGHTER in my four years at college. I had to write an eight-page paper on Charlotte Perkins Gilman's short story "The Yellow Wallpaper" for an English class. The day before it was due, I locked myself in my dorm room around 9 p.m. and began typing. About 10 Cokes and eight hours later, I saw the sun rise outside my window. I will never forget feeling that tired. The paper was terrible. I swore that was my last all-nighter.

—AMY
WETHERSFIELD, CONNECTICUT

DEPRIVED (NOT DRUNK) GETS A "D"

You probably already know in a general sense that staying up all night isn't good for you, but there's also evidence that staying up all night to study will not be good for your academic performance. Recent research shows that when people are sleep deprived, their minds simply don't work very well. In fact, one study found that sleep-deprived medical students performed as poorly on a variety of measures as they would have if they were well rested—but drunk! You would, I hope, never knock back a few beers before going to take your sociology final exam: If the University of Michigan study is correct, consistently depriving yourself of the rest you need is almost as bad.

INSTEAD OF LOSING SLEEP, I say, *get* some sleep. If you have a big paper to write, go to bed as soon as you get home, even if it's 5 p.m. Then wake up in time to write, and you'll be more alert.

—ERIN VAUGHN
CHICAGO, ILLINOIS
WASHINGTON UNIVERSITY IN ST. LOUIS GPA: 3.76

RECIPES FOR SUCCESS

WHEN I HAVE EXAMS, I write a "recipe" for each one; it's my little secret. I take a sheet of paper for each exam and make a list of everything I need to study, in what order, and for how long. I consider these the steps to follow in the recipe, and the study materials are the ingredients. If I follow the recipe, as in a making a cake, I end up with success— although a cake would be much better!

—LAUREN MICHELLE SHER
GAINESVILLE, FLORIDA
UNIVERSITY OF FLORIDA GPA: 3.86

• • • • • • • •

RECIPE FOR AN ALL-NIGHTER: Work out for an hour to get your endorphins going. Next, have a cup of coffee. Then, take a 20-minute nap and by the time you wake up, the coffee will have kicked in and you can begin studying or writing your paper. Enjoy many sugary snacks throughout the night, and drink lots of water so you'll have to get up and go to the bathroom, an activity that will help keep you alert.

—MICHELLE WADDELL
HOLLYWOOD, FLORIDA
WASHINGTON UNIVERSITY IN ST. LOUIS GPA: 3.38

MY FRESHMAN YEAR I was living in the dorms and had a huge exam at 8 a.m. I had spent the entire night studying and planned to go to bed at exactly 11 p.m. the night before, so I would be refreshed to take the test. On this particular night, however, some jokers, who were most likely drunk, decided to pull the fire alarm; not once, not twice, but three times at various points during the night and early morning. And each time I had to get out of bed and go outside (did I mention that it was winter?). It worked out though, because since I couldn't sleep I ended up studying more!

—ZACHARY URNESS
POLSON, MONTANA
UNIVERSITY OF ST. THOMAS

• • • • • • • •

PRACTICE GOOD HYGIENE, even when you're cramming. My freshman year, I was studying all weekend for my chemistry midterm (I hadn't done any of the reading all semester). I just plopped myself at my desk and didn't get up. I didn't shower at all and just hid my longish hair under a baseball hat. Sunday evening, I took my hat off and looked at myself in the mirror; my hair had gotten so greasy it was clumping together. I was so disgusted, I cut my mane the next day.

—M.J.
HOBOKEN, NEW JERSEY
UNIVERSITY OF PENNSYLVANIA

I STUDIED ALL NIGHT with a partner for the midterm. In the morning we took a half-hour break to go back to our own rooms and get ready for class. In that half hour, we both fell asleep! We both missed the midterm!

—MELISSA BERMAN
MANALAPAN, NEW JERSY
MUHLENBERG COLLEGE GPA: 3.92

* * * * * * * *

My friend stayed up all night studying: she was so tired in class, she fell over and cracked her head open. She had to go to the hospital and didn't get her project done.

—S.S.
CURLEW, WASHINGTON
WASHINGTON UNIVERSITY IN ST. LOUIS

* * * * * * * *

I PERFORM BEST WHEN I wake up early to finish work. I'm always fresher after even a short night's sleep. You need to give your mind and body a break from the stresses and fatigue due to long hours of studying.

—SAMUEL
PALO ALTO, CALIFORNIA
STANFORD UNIVERSITY

AT ONE POINT DURING MY SENIOR YEAR I was planning on staying fairly late to do some work, but I got so caught up in studying that I neglected to hear the last bell ring to close the library. Once 3 a.m. rolled around, I found I was stuck in the library for the night. There was nothing else to do but plow through the rest of my work. I was fortified by an immense quiet, the occasional spooky sound, and hourly breaks to flip through some random Aristotle books in the stacks. My friends thought I was dead, but I got an A on the paper and the test!

—JESSE MCCREE
SOMERVILLE, MASSACHUSETTS
BOWDOIN COLLEGE GPA: 3.6

* * * * * * * *

I LIKE MY SLEEP, so I don't pull all-nighters. I would rather go in to a test rested and know less. The more information I have stored in my brain, the more stressed out I get. Most of my tests are essay tests. I think if you study too much you end up writing way too much; you try to regurgitate all the information you stored in your head from the night before. By just learning the main points, you are able to write clear and organized essays. I end up looking like I know more than someone who studied every single detail.

—LAURA GORDON
ASPEN, COLORADO
UNIVERSITY OF CALIFORNIA, LOS ANGELES GPA: 3.2

Studying for a test a couple of hours before is called cramming; but two days before the test is called ample preparation!

—BRENDA-GAIL
MARIE CORLEY
CHICAGO,
ILLINOIS
SOUTHERN
ILLINOIS
UNIVERSITY

FRAN'S FABLES: THREE CREPUSCULAR CREATURES

Crepuscular creatures are animals that come out to hunt or forage at twilight. Early one evening the moose, the mouse, and the rabbit met for breakfast just as the sun was setting.

"I love to watch the sunset," sighed the mouse.

"Not too bright, not too dark," observed the moose.

"Well, I agree," said the rabbit, "but don't you ever wonder what the world is like at night?"

"That's when we sleep," replied the mouse, starting to get worried.

"One night without sleep won't hurt us. Come on, let's stay out tonight and see what it's all about. I bet we'll learn a lot."

Eventually the other two agreed. The next evening, they watched the sunset as usual, but instead of heading off to bed soon afterward they took a trip to the riverbank.

"Wow," said the rabbit, "look at how the flowers fold in on themselves after dark! We have to remember this."

They wandered around the human elementary school. "There are no children here at night," the mouse noticed. "We can go wherever we please. We have to remember that."

They discovered an uncovered garbage can in an alley behind a busy restaurant. "The people are rushing around so much in there, they probably forget the lid all the time," commented the rabbit as they snacked. "We have to remember this."

The animals made many exciting discoveries that night, and vowed to remember them all. They enjoyed their roaming so much that the sun was rising again before they returned home, exhausted.

It took several days of catching up on sleep before the friends got together again. "That was some night we had," said the moose.

"It's funny, but I got so tired, I don't really remember where we went," mused the rabbit.

"I don't remember where we went either," said the mouse, "but I know it was fun going there with you."

The moral of the story: The only reason to pull an all-nighter is to share a bonding experience with your friends.

AS A FRESHMAN, the idea of pulling an all-nighter seemed to be the only way to ace a test. But I quickly learned that this was not the case. I had a biology test to take, the last exam before the final, so I was under a lot of pressure. The night before the test, I pulled an all-nighter. The day of the test, I felt as though my hard work paid off. Then I got my grade. The grade was definitely not worth an all-nighter.

—ANONYMOUS
MIAMI, FLORIDA
UNIVERSITY OF MIAMI

. . . .

I STAYED UP TO STUDY for my calculus final. I started studying around 4 p.m. the day before and stayed up until my exam time at 8 a.m. As soon as I finished my exam, I went to a bar with my friends and ended up partying until the next day at 9 a.m. That's when I finally crashed.

—BRETT
FT. LEE, NEW JERSEY
PENNSYLVANIA STATE UNIVERSITY

. . . .

EVERY ONCE IN A WHILE you have to go a night or two without sleeping. I used to miss one night a week, but luckily my problem sets were due at the end of the week so I would miss my night on a Thursday night and have the weekend to catch up.

—JONATHAN GARDNER
YREKA, CALIFORNIA
CALIFORNIA INSTITUTE OF TECHNOLOGY

Zoom In: Choosing a Major

When I started college, I was absolutely sure about what I wanted to major in: studio art. I took drawing and painting and art history, plus a random assortment of interesting electives, but no solid introductory courses in other disciplines. Why should I? I didn't need to explore. I had a plan. Except that I realized after three or four semesters that I didn't have the motivation to stay up all night in the studio like the other art majors. Things just weren't clicking any more.

It was time for a change. I switched to English because I never got tired of reading books, or talking and writing about them. And to this day, I still haven't gotten tired of working with language.

"What does this have to do with me?" you may be wondering. Essentially, I want you to know that it's OK to take some time (not infinite time, but some) to decide on a major. If all your friends seem to know already what they want to study, you can rest assured that 50 percent are not as sure as they look, and 25 percent more will end up changing their major later. The remaining 25 percent may really know, but that's not your problem.

Take the time to explore various academic disciplines in school. Outside of class, investigate a range of career fields by going to job fairs and panel discussions, and by seeking out internships and shadowing experiences. You can also read career-focused magazines and web sites.

Psychologists say that the condition of uncertainty is one of the hardest conditions for human beings to bear. I know that the temptation to declare a major—maybe any major!— just to feel some security, can be strong. But there are around 30,000 different jobs that people do in the U.S. If you sat down right now and listed all the jobs you could think of, I'm sure you would have nowhere near 30,000. Within that vast number there must be fields that you don't know about. One of those unknown fields might be perfect for you—if you take the time and put in the effort to find it.

MY ORIGINAL PLAN was to be a cell biologist. I had taken three years of biology and chemistry in college. But I took a very tough cellular biology class my junior year and received a D. I decided to change my major to advertising because I would need the least number of credits in that major to graduate on time. I loved science, but by that point in college I realized that I didn't love it as much as the rest of my fellow students. I don't regret my decision. I went into graphic design and I'm very happy with my career.

—MICHELE
ROCKAWAY TOWNSHIP, NEW JERSEY
BOSTON UNIVERSITY

• • • • • • • •

AT LEAST THREE-QUARTERS of my friends changed their majors before graduation. I entered Marquette majoring in international business, but switched during my sophomore year to a double major in economics and political science. I didn't want to take the rigorous accounting classes required of sophomore business students, and I realized that you don't need to major in international business to work with global commerce. Also, I planned to go on to postgraduate business school, where I'd gain exposure to this information when it was much more applicable for my career.

—SAM WEAVER
MINNEAPOLIS, MINNESOTA
MARQUETTE UNIVERSITY

WHEN YOU ALREADY KNOW

I WAS INVOLVED WITH MY HIGH SCHOOL newspaper and never questioned that that's what I'd do. I knew I liked to write, and that seemed the best way to do it and make money. Granted, it's not a lot of money, but it's enough to live and let me do what I love. That's probably the best way to choose if you're unsure. Find something you love, that you don't consider work, and figure out how to get paid to do it.

—JACLYN YOUHANA
LIBERTY TOWNSHIP, OHIO

. . . .

I THOUGHT I WANTED TO BE A TEACHER; I was always sitting my brothers and sisters in front of me while I read to them. But my junior year in high school, I took an accounting class; it changed my life. My accounting teacher said I could become a CPA, an auditor, even a consultant, and make lots of money, and set my own hours. Who would have thought? And I didn't even like math.

—EVETTE WILLIS
CHICAGO, ILLINOIS
CHICAGO STATE UNIVERSITY

A LOT OF PEOPLE FOCUS too much on a career goal and not enough on what interests them. Or they do the opposite: they put too much emphasis on what courses fascinate them, and not enough on what kind of job they'll actually be qualified for when they graduate. My sister majored in sociology, which she loved, but after college she tried sales and then teaching but wasn't happy doing either one, and she's still trying to find the right niche.

—AMY
TAMPA, FLORIDA
WASHINGTON UNIVERSITY IN ST. LOUIS

* * * * * * * *

I chose mass communications, with a focus on public relations, because I can't be tied down to a computer all day. I want to talk to people, make them feel good, ease their nerves, and take any chance to get in front of the camera.

—ANONYMOUS
CHICAGO, ILLINOIS

WHEN CHOOSING A MAJOR, especially if you are planning to go to graduate school, remember that it's much better to get A's in a more prestigious major than in what some schools would term a "blow-off" major. Find the most challenging subject that you like and can do well in. I chose molecular cell biology because I've liked biology since high school. It's one of the more difficult majors at UC Berkeley, so I know that If I do really well in it, then any graduate school I apply to will say: here's someone who did exceptionally well in a subject that is really hard.

—MICHAEL POWELL
GLENDALE, CALIFORNIA
UNIVERSTIY OF CALIFORNIA, BERKELEY GPA: 3.63

Never enter college thinking you have it all planned out. It's good to have an idea, but it's better to leave it open for other opportunities when they present themselves (because they will).

—RACHEL ALDRICH
BROOKLYN PARK, MINNESOTA
UNIVERSITY OF WISCONSIN, GPA: 3.7

I REALLY LIKED MATH, but I wanted to be more marketable, so I majored in finance. Once I started taking some economic courses, I liked it so much that I majored in that, too. And I still graduated in four years since I also took summer classes. I found a job right after.

—KENDRA GONZALEZ
SCHAUMBURG, ILLINOIS
UNIVERSITY OF ILLINOIS

. . . .

I CHOSE TO MAJOR IN ENGLISH at UCLA, because my native languages are French and Vietnamese and I wanted to improve my English. I want to stay in the United States and go to law school here, so it was really important for me to learn the language. I would tell anyone who asked to choose a major that will help them with their future career plans.

—F.T.
LOS ANGELES, CALIFORNIA
UNIVERSITY OF CALIFORNIA, LOS ANGELES

. . . .

I CHOSE AN INTERDISCIPLINARY major so I could take courses in lots of departments.

M.K.
BROOKYN PARK, MINNESOTA
BELOIT COLLEGE

I wanted to major in pop culture, but my dad said I'd never get a job. So, I decided to major in journalism, too.

—ANNA
NEW YORK,
NEW YORK
BOWLING
GREEN STATE
UNIVERSITY
GPA: 3.74

I'VE WANTED TO DO COMPUTER SCIENCE since I was 10. Since I have one shot to be here at Berkeley doing computer science, I'm going to make my mark in these courses, which are renowned around the country. I'm determined to take something out of this school and at the same time I am going to love doing it. I guess you can say I'm attached to my major. I just want to take advantage of a situation I am lucky to be in, one that I will never have again.

—BRIAN
BABYLON, NEW YORK
UNIVERSITY OF CALIFORNIA, BERKELEY

• • • • • • • • •

IN YOUR FRESHMAN YEAR, take a few courses in different areas and see what suits you best. That way you can make a decision before your sophomore year and sign up for courses you'll need for that degree. Talk to professors in different departments. They may help you find graduates who will let you shadow them at their jobs. It's real-world experiences like that that can help you make the right decision. Let's face it: you don't know how a profession is going to be until you learn the ins and outs of the business.

—JENNIFER STOUT
BONFIELD, ILLINOIS
OLIVET NAZARENE UNIVERSITY

FIVE BAD REASONS FOR GOING PREMED—AND SOME GOOD REASONS

BAD

1. You laugh your head off during every episode of *Scrubs*.
2. Your friends and family are really impressed when you tell them you are going to be a doctor.
3. You have wanted to be a doctor ever since you were in kindergarten, and you have never considered any other option. Only losers change their minds.
4. It's all about the Benjamins, right?
5. You would look great in a white coat.

GOOD

1. You've been volunteering in a medical setting for years. You see what doctors do on a daily basis and you can't wait to step into that role yourself.
2. You have a strong aptitude for science, compassion, and great communication skills.
3. You're not sure what field of medicine you want to go into, but you get good grades in science, so you adopt a basic premed curriculum to keep your options open while you explore.

I KNEW I WANTED TO DO something with science and I knew I liked to work on things like cars and bikes, so mechanical engineering seemed the obvious choice. However, when I chose the major I didn't really understand the job of an engineer. Ask anyone what an engineer does and they will most likely say, "They make something from nothing." I used to think that, until I started taking classes and learned that an engineer is just a small part of this very huge process of designing something.

—TREVOR EDMONDS
BERKELEY, CALIFORNIA
UNIVERSITY OF CALIFORNIA, BERKELEY GPA: 3.5

• • • • • • • •

I LOVED TO WRITE, so I knew that I wanted to do something that had to do with writing; I just wasn't sure what that was. I was in the college of general studies, and for the first two years, you take core courses that you don't necessarily want to take. After that, I went into the college of communications, chose print journalism, and narrowed it down to magazine feature writing.

—A.K.
POUND RIDGE, NEW YORK
BOSTON COLLEGE

You usually have to choose your major before the end of your sophomore year, which comes quickly. You have barely any time to think it over.

—BRIDGET SCRABECK
LAKEVILLE, MINNESOTA
UNIVERSITY OF ST. THOMAS

I SWITCHED FROM ASTROPHYSICS to anthropology after my freshman year. In high school I did well in physics, so I figured I would do astrophysics. But when I was in class in college, I didn't care about what the professor was saying. Don't be afraid to change everything and search for what you like the most. I have more homework now, but I do better grade-wise because I care about it.

—JON WALDO
NASHVILLE, TENNESSEE
BOSTON UNIVERSITY

• • • • • • • •

CHOOSE A MAJOR ON A SUBJECT you know something about. Choose something you love and something you want to expand your knowledge of. I am from Baghdad and I always liked the English language. I never had to study and I always did well. So when I graduated from high school in Baghdad, I just knew I wanted to study English. I majored in English in undergraduate school and now I am getting my master's degree in journalism.

—OMAR FEKEIKI
BERKELEY, CALIFORNIA
ALTURATH UNIVERSITY COLLEGE, BAGHDAD

FIVE BAD REASONS FOR GOING PRELAW—AND SOME GOOD REASONS

BAD

1. You love watching courtroom dramas on TV.
2. Your friends and family are really impressed when you tell them you're going to be a lawyer.
3. You love to argue!
4. You've heard it's a great way to make money without working too hard.
5. Other than medicine, what other profession is there?

GOOD

1. You have a gift for language; in performing close, detailed analysis of texts, and in writing clear, strong arguments.
2. You have shadowed a lawyer or interned in a law office, and it just feels right.
3. You are consistently fascinated by a certain area of law, such as intellectual property.
4. You are looking for a strong foundation for a career in public service.

I CAME HERE THINKING I was going to do one thing and now I'm almost certain I'll be doing another. That's the great thing about college; you can always change your mind and do something else. Don't worry if you don't know what to major in. Just by being on a college campus you will be exposed to subjects you didn't even know existed, and eventually something will interest you.

—LIZETTE CARDENAS
LOS ANGELES, CALIFORNIA
UNIVERSITY OF CALIFORNIA, LOS ANGELES GPA: 3.3

* * * * * * * *

My nursing program was only two years, and then I was guaranteed a job. Hospitals are begging for nurses. I didn't want to be like those people majoring in creative writing, and waitressing afterwards,

—A.P.
CHICAGO, ILLINOIS
MALCOLM X COLLEGE

WHEN GOALS DIFFER

What do you do if you want to study theater, but your parents want you to be a doctor? Or if your parents expect you to get an MBA and join the family business, but you just can't see yourself being happy in that life?

I have worked with many students torn between the wish to please their families and their own convictions about the path their lives should take. This is a very tough situation. Some students come from cultures where children are expected to obey their parents in all things, and to do otherwise is thought to show lack of love or respect. Some students have been told that they will be cut off financially if they don't fall in line.

If you have a good relationship with your academic advisor, let him or her know what you are dealing with. The counseling center at your school can also help you by giving you a safe place to express feelings about the conflict with your family, and assist you in developing strategies for seeking some common ground.

Here are some ideas you can begin with:

- If your parents have one career in mind but you want to do something else, prepare a presentation on your desired field. Research prospects, average starting salaries, and typical benefits.

- If your parents are eager to see you declare a "practical" major but you're not ready, research different majors at your college. Show your parents how course requirements work at your school—prove that it's possible to graduate in four years even if you take time to explore.
- Don't reject an academic field just because your parents are pushing it on you. Try a course or two in that area—you might like it after all. At least your parents will see that you gave it your best shot.
- No matter how cogent your arguments, you might need to bring in some extra support in the form of someone older—an aunt or uncle, a professor, or a family friend—your parents will listen to.
- If you and your parents can't come to an agreement, you can always try a double major, or a major and a minor—one for them, one for you.
- See your college career counselor. With some creative vocational exploration, you may be able to find a career that bridges what you want to do and what your parents want you to do.

I THOUGHT I WOULD ENJOY social work because I was a troubled youth: I wanted to intervene during children's early years, so they wouldn't have to sing the same song I did. But once I started taking courses, the professors and the books drove me from it, because social work seemed more scientific and political rather than social. I switched to liberal arts.

—ANONYMOUS
RICHTON PARK, ILLINOIS

• • • • • • • • •

I CHOSE MY MAJOR BECAUSE my cousin was an electrical engineer and he said not only was it fun, but the money was good. Plus, my college offered me a four-year scholarship to get more African-American girls into the program. It was an offer I couldn't refuse.

—CORAVIECE TERRY
MOUNDS, ILLINOIS
🏛 SOUTHERN ILLINOIS UNIVERSITY, CARBONDALE

• • • • • • • • •

TAKE A VARIETY OF COURSES your freshman year if you're not sure what your major will be. You can always make up credit hours during summers if you find yourself behind. And even if a major seems hard, if it's your passion, do it! You're more likely to make the grades and succeed if you're doing something you really love.

—MANDY TAKACS
MEDINA, OHIO
🏛 BOWLING GREEN STATE UNIVERSITY

I WAS ALWAYS REALLY GOOD in math so I just gravitated towards math as a major. I'm at law school now and I think the math major prepared me well. Any sort of academic application of your thoughts can prepare you for law school, or any graduate school. Even if you are planning on a career in writing or history, or anything for that matter, math helps you think in terms of principles and fundamentals.

—Arthur Lechtholz-Zey
Los Angeles, California
University of California, Los Angeles

* * * * * * * *

I WENT WITH RADIO and television production because I'm a visual learner. I knew that classes wouldn't be the typical lectures, where I'm listening to some professor read the book word for word. I knew it would consist of hands-on work, like running the video camera, or putting a set together. Any other major, and I probably wouldn't have made it through college.

—Cedric Malone
Carbondale, Illinois
Southern Illinois University

* * * * * * * *

I MAJORED IN CLASSICS because it was the unconventional choice.

—M.K.
Brooklyn Park, Minnesota
Beloit College

Consider

IF YOU CHOOSE A MAJOR just because you hope it will lead to a high-paying career, you won't do as well in school. Choose a field you're passionate about; you'll be happier and make better grades. I found out there are plenty of ways to make a good living in my chosen field of theater: directing, lighting, producing, or teaching. Not just acting.

—JAMIE LARSON
ST. LOUIS, MISSOURI
TRUMAN STATE UNIVERSITY

• • • • • • • •

I MAJORED IN BIOLOGY because I wanted to be a doctor after seeing medical dramas and sitcoms on television. The doctor was always the star. But I lost the desire to study, and I hated attending class; I knew there was more to being a doctor than watching *ER* and *Doogie Howser*. I changed my major to radio and television, and never looked back.

—KARINNE SPENCER
CHICAGO, ILLINOIS
SOUTHERN ILLINOIS UNIVERSITY

• • • • • • • •

I THOUGHT IT WAS IMPORTANT to go outside of what I was good at. If I picked a major that was more challenging to me I would get more out of my studies than if I just chose something that I was good at to begin with.

—BRIDGET SCRABECK
LAKEVILLE, MINNESOTA
UNIVERSITY OF ST. THOMAS

I CHOSE ELEMENTARY EDUCATION because teaching children is something that I knew I would enjoy. It may not bring in a whole lot of money, but I don't hate going to work every day, plus I have my summers off, and I don't have to worry about being laid off just because stockholders want bigger dividends.

—CARLA MANNING
CHICAGO, ILLINOIS
UNIVERSITY OF GEORGIA

. . . .

A LOT OF STUDENTS CONFUSE higher education with job training. You major in something that interests you; something you enjoy. Almost any major will give you the same end result in terms of career. I chose to major in Latin and I'm thinking of going into law enforcement. College gives you the tools and the critical thinking skills you need to go out into the world, and you can get that from any major.

—JACK LIGMAN
LANCASTER, CALIFORNIA
UNIVERSITY OF CALIFORNIA, LOS ANGELES

. . . .

DO SOME RESEARCH about the profession you want to go into someday: that way, when you do graduate from college, you will know the probability of getting a job in that field, or if you will have to go on for further education.

—RACHEL ALDRICH
BROOKLYN PARK, MINNESOTA
UNIVERSITY OF WISCONSIN GPA: 3.7

WHEN I WENT TO COLLEGE I was pretty sure I was going to be a history major. I automatically took courses I needed to fulfill those requirements. By my sophomore year I realized I wasn't very happy with history. I didn't like the courses and how competitive people were. I took a couple of courses in fine arts and really loved them. I'm a fine arts major now. I wish I had taken a wide array of courses in various fields the first semesters, instead of focusing so narrowly; I wish my advisors had stressed that more.

—JOHN KEELEY
MORRISTOWN, NEW JERSEY
HARVARD UNIVERSITY

. . . .

IF YOU ARE GOING TO CHOOSE a competitive field to go into, like journalism, where you are not being offered a signing bonus for an entry-level position, please be the best. Don't think that just because you got a degree, the *Chicago Tribune* will be knocking on your door. If you don't like to work hard, choose a major with the most guarantees.

—MELISSA BERNARD
COUNTRY CLUB HILLS, ILLINOIS
COLUMBIA COLLEGE

One to One: Relationships with Your Professors

Much of what I do as an academic advisor is based on what I wish someone had told me when I was a college student. I can't tell you how many times I have wished that someone had told me how important it was to form long-term academic relationships with professors. Maybe someone did tell me, or I read it in a pamphlet; if so, it never sank in. As a result, I never made it a point to take multiple classes with the same professor; I never went to office hours just to chat about the course material; and I had a hard time when, as a senior, I had to think about whom to ask for letters of recommendation.

Out of all the suggestions I make in this book, this is one of the most important—and the most difficult. After all, you can implement study techniques in the privacy of your home or the library. You can research majors on the Internet. Even the decision to embrace academic integrity takes place inside your own conscience. But forming relationships with your professors forces you to move outside your comfort zone. Professors sometimes seem intimidating or unapproachable; taking the first step may not be easy for you, especially if you are on the shy side, or never talked much with your high school teachers.

I understand how you may feel about taking on this project, and I will not leave you hanging! Throughout this section, I will provide tips on how to take your first steps in connecting with your professors. Once you get started, the benefits will begin pouring in, and you will have more than enough motivation to keep going.

GETTING TO KNOW YOUR PROFESSORS might not seem important now, but those relationships will come in handy when you need a recommendation for a job or grad school application. The best way to get to know a professor is to work on a project where he or she is the advisor, and be able to get a real sense of your personality and passion for your work. Attending office hours once in a while also helps. Spending that extra hour a week will make for a more personal and detailed recommendation.

—JACOB SZE
ELLENVILLE, NEW YORK
CORNELL UNIVERSITY

YOU CAN END UP BECOMING great friends with some of your professors, and they become your advisors, able to give you recommendations for after college as well. One of my English teachers helped me out with an independent study project during senior year. We still e-mail back and forth. She gives me general advice on what I'm working on and career advice. I had questions concerning possible career choices, and she has been able to give me guidance.

—ELIZABETH
MOORESTOWN, NEW JERSEY
FAIRFIELD UNIVERSITY

PRACTICAL APPLICATION

When I was a freshman I knew I wanted to participate in a program my college offers to spend a semester in Washington, D.C. While there, I wanted to intern for the national news show, *The McLaughlin Group*. As soon as I could, I introduced myself to the head of my department and told her my plans. When it was time for me to go to Washington, she helped by granting college credit for it. Getting to know my professors also helped later on when I was faced with taking a mandatory class on journalism theory when I wanted to do something more practical and hands-on. I approached my professor, with whom I had already developed a relationship, and asked if I could substitute the class with one on broadcast journalism. He agreed, but I'm not sure it would have gone as smoothly if the first time I had ever spoken to him outside of class had been to ask him for a favor.

—JASON PAUL TORREANO
LOCKPORT, NEW YORK
STATE UNIVERSITY OF NEW YORK, BROCKPORT

I ADMIRE SOME OF MY FEMALE science professors. Not only do they juggle cutting-edge science research, but they also have time to raise a family and teach classes, and be there for me! It inspires me to keep working hard to realize my goals. I aspire to be one of those women.

—Nicole Spence
Atlanta, Georgia
Emory University GPA: 3.71

THE PROFESSOR WHO ENDED UP being my favorite was one of the most hated professors in the English department. He would find people who hadn't done the reading, and embarrass the hell out of them. I was so scared to *not* do the work that I ended up learning more in that class than any other.

—Zachary Urness
Polson, Montana
University of St. Thomas

I CAME OUT WITH AMAZING relationships with my professors and I was able to feed off of their enthusiasm. Everyone has that one professor who really gets them motivated. Getting to know someone like that in my department gave me the opportunity to learn other things outside of class. I really had my eyes open to real life.

—Tim
Santa Cruz, California
Sonoma State University

WORST PROFESSORS EVER

I TOOK A CLASS CALLED MADNESS IN LITERATURE. The teacher was the strangest professor I've ever encountered. At first I took his peculiarity as good, but it ended up being bizarre. He always wore a three-piece suit with some kind of bow tie. He would come into class and take off his long coat and carefully fold it over his chair. He was very anal about where everything belonged. He made comments and I was never sure if he was joking or serious. I was never sure about what my papers were supposed to be about. I tried to meet him during office hours and I still couldn't get it. He just had no social skills and made me uncomfortable. I wish I'd never taken the class.

—YINKA
CLINTON, MARYLAND
UNIVERSITY OF PENNSYLVANIA

• • • • • • • •

IN MY 150-STUDENT PSYCHOLOGY 101 COURSE, the professor was unreachable. He was like a celebrity, and the TAs were his bodyguards. If you tried to walk to toward him after class to ask questions about the midterm, a TA would meet you halfway with folded arms. The TA's look forced me to turn the other way. I just had to rely on my memory to pass the tests.

—JAMAE TERRY
ST. LOUIS, MISSOURI
SOUTHERN ILLINOIS UNIVERSITY, CARBONDALE

MY WORST PROFESSOR was my organizational communications professor, who was also my academic advisor. At the beginning of class, she told us that we had a better chance of winning the lottery than getting an A out of her class. She even disagreed on a lot of the theories in the assigned book. So when I wrote a paper, I didn't know what to do; agree with her, agree with the book, or make up my own theory. I got a C. I knew I didn't deserve it, but she was my academic advisor and I wanted to graduate on time.

—SYREETA BURNETT
WHEATON, ILLINOIS
DEPAUL UNIVERSITY

· · · · · · · · ·

I KNEW SOMETHING WAS WRONG with my managerial economics professor after I flunked his class, took his course again and was still failing; and so was most of the class. I would ask him a question and he would always say, "Catch me after class, we have to move on." After class he would be gone. When enough students complained that he didn't know how to teach his subject, the school did a background check on him and discovered that he lied on his resumé; he didn't have a Master's degree, which was required to teach the course. I finally passed the course.

—ANONYMOUS
CHICAGO, ILLINOIS

BEST PROFESSORS EVER

MME. ROCHAT, THE STUDY-ABROAD COORDINATOR for my junior year in Paris, is one of the most incredible professors I have had. She organized trips and excursions for us, made sure we were happy with our host families, corrected our papers, and took a personal interest in each of the students under her care. When Thanksgiving came, she made a traditional Thanksgiving dinner for all of us in her tiny Parisian apartment. In spring, she helped many of us (including me) get fellowships so that we could spend the rest of the summer in France.

—LAURA CARROLL
SALEM, MASSACHUSETTS
SMITH COLLEGE

• • • • • • • •

MY FAVORITE PROFESSOR IS IN THE HISTORY and humanities department. He's classic: He wears a tweed blazer, white hat, and argyle sweater. I took a course with him called European Thought and Culture. We read Marx, Locke and Rousseau. As a side interest, he writes all of these books on gay culture today, so I think he's a really cool dude. And since I'm a history major, I get to visit him during his office hours to talk to him and get advice from someone I respect.

—ANONYMOUS
NEW YORK, NEW YORK
STANFORD UNIVERSITY GPA: 3.7

THE MAN WHO REALLY INSPIRED ME to finish books was my comparative literature professor. He taught classes on Nabokov, Dostoyevsky, and Gogol that were actually fun. Any man who can breathe life into *The Brothers Karamazov* is all right by me.

—JONATHAN
BROOKLYN, NEW YORK

• • • • • • • •

MY FRESHMAN POLITICAL SCIENCE PROFESSOR was genuinely interested in teaching us about American government and politics. He was easy to talk to if something was unclear or if you had a question about a grade. He is my hero because he helped me enjoy my first semester in college and to major in political science.

—ERICA
HOUSTON, TEXAS
SYRACUSE UNIVERSITY GPA: 3.3

• • • • • • • •

MY FAVORITE PROFESSOR WAS THIS NUTTY GUY who taught Intro to Popular Culture. He would wear his pants legs rolled up in winter for no reason and would use the beak of a rubber chicken instead of a pointer in class. For the first time in his class, I started to see things in a larger context, which is what college is for.

—ANNA
NEW YORK, NEW YORK
BOWLING GREEN STATE UNIVERSITY GPA: 3.74

MY FAVORITE PROFESSOR TAUGHT CALCULUS 1, 2, and 3, and she was determined that I pass her classes. She would come to the study sessions in the dorms, she would expand her office hours, and she would even take me to lunch. One time a student became sick for several weeks, and she brought the homework to her house. She always said that if she was blessed to be a professor, she would do anything to make students achieve their goals. She lived up to her motto. I was more than a student to her; I was a person.

—CORAVIECE TERRY
MOUNDS, ILLINOIS
SOUTHERN ILLINOIS UNIVERSITY, CARBONDALE

• • • • • • • • •

DR. DAVID BLOOMQUIST HAS BEEN my favorite professor for several reasons: First, I am a very serious student and he was the goofiest professor I have ever had. He would always start class by showing us something not related to the material, such as funny Internet videos or his electric dog. Second, he would lecture for half the class time, and I always, *always* learned the material. His personality is the complete opposite of mine. His tests and homework were never easy but I always wanted to do well: I wanted him to remember me, although he probably doesn't.

—LAUREN MICHELLE SHER
GAINESVILLE, FLORIDA
UNIVERSITY OF FLORIDA GPA: 3.86

I HAVE ONE PROFESSOR who might end up my mentor. She's trying to convince me to go into human biology. This professor has her own lab funded by the National Institutes of Health. She has a ton of resources and she's cited in our textbooks. It is just really cool to have kind of famous people as professors.

—MARIA
MORAGO, CALIFORNIA
STANFORD UNIVERSITY

. . . .

I WAS ONLY CLOSE WITH ONE OF MY PROFESSORS, but she was great. She taught me how to be a reporter. She told me that I was too good a writer to waste it on advertising and that I should seriously consider changing my major to journalism and pursuing it as a career.

—ANDREW SHAFER
NEW YORK, NEW YORK
IOWA STATE UNIVERSITY GPA: 3.34

. . . .

MY ENGLISH TEACHER MADE US write notes to her on the last day of class so she would have something to remember each one of us. She was very emotional; she wanted us to know how easy it is to forget things once they are out of sight.

—SONIA MENDOZA
LOS ANGELES, CALIFORNIA
UNIVERSITY OF CALIFORNIA, LOS ANGELES

THERE'S A LECTURER IN PHYSICS who is technically a graduate student, but he's a tenured graduate student. He's the only guy who knows how to make the stuff in the Physics 6 and 7 labs work. He is a retired commander in the Navy and I am Air Force R.O.T.C., so that established an immediate bond. When you can talk to someone about how you're doing, how to change things and how to make things better then it is much easier to make things better, as opposed to having to suffer through it and being someone who can't get mercy if necessary.

—J.G.
MANITOU SPRINGS, COLORADO
CALIFORNIA INSTITUTE OF TECHNOLOGY GPA: 3.5

• • • • • • • •

I HAD ONE PROFESSOR MY SOPHOMORE YEAR who approached his subject with such wild-eyed enthusiasm and passion that it was hard to think of him doing anything other than teaching this subject. He took a normally placid subject—post-Civil War history—and got us students to think it was the most important thing in the world. That's the best kind of professor I can think of.

—JESSE MCCREE
SOMERVILLE, MASSACHUSETTS
BOWDOIN COLLEGE GPA: 3.6

I CURRENTLY STALK ONE OF MY TAs because I'm not doing well in the class and I need his help all of the time. His dorm is right near mine so I'll usually just pop over there and say, "Hi, didn't know you would be here, lucky to run into you, I need help with problem set number four!" After a few unannounced visits he said that instead of just popping up, I should set up some meetings with him where he would gladly help me.

—LAUREN
HAWTHORNE, CALIFORNIA
STANFORD UNIVERSITY GPA: 3.5

IN UPPER-DIVISION COURSES, professors care more and give you the benefit of the doubt more than in lower-division classes. The courses are smaller and they understand that the people in the class want to be there. At this level, they can be both your friend and your instructor.

—MICHAEL ABRAMOVITZ
ALTA LOMA, CALIFORNIA
UNIVERSITY OF ARIZONA GPA: 2.65

- - - - - - - - -

My instructors can't tell us everything they know about a subject in class, so I like to pick their brains outside of class.

—ROB J. METZLER
BUFFALO, NEW YORK
STATE UNIVERSITY OF NEW YORK, BUFFALO

- - - - - - - - -

GETTING TO KNOW YOUR PROFESSORS can help with grades as well as other perks. One of my professors, who was also my advisor, recommended me as a student representative to review my major with officials from the university. I got to offer personal input into what I thought was good and bad with the program.

—MANDY TAKACS
MEDINA, OHIO
BOWLING GREEN STATE UNIVERSITY

NO BUDDY

ON A PROFESSOR'S 55TH BIRTHDAY, my friend wished her a happy birthday and gleefully commented, "You're officially a senior citizen!" The teacher did not think that was a compliment. I like to schmooze with my teachers about skiing and such. I try to read them and figure out what they're like. Whether it's common politics or interests, I think it helps the teacher remember you better and puts you on their good side.

—LAURA GLASS
GOLDEN VALLEY, MINNESOTA
UNIVERSITY OF ST. THOMAS

• • • • • • • • •

I HAVE OBSERVED THAT NO MATTER how buddy-buddy your professor seems, she is *not* your sorority sister. He is *not* your fraternity brother. They are higher powers, believe it or not, and they don't need to see you in "party mode." Bottom line: If you and a professor or assistant are out at the same drinking establishment, keep a low profile. Smile, say hi. Don't offer a drink, don't talk about class, just pass on by.

—KATHLEEN MCDONALD
TROY, MICHIGAN
MICHIGAN STATE UNIVERSITY

OFFICE HOURS!

PREPARE YOUR QUESTIONS before you go to a professor's office hours. I've gone into office hours without a clear mind and felt completely put off by my professor. Avoid feeling embarrassed and know exactly what you want to say before you go in.

—DANNY J. HERRERA
LYNWOOD, CALIFORNIA
UNIVERSITY OF CALIFORNIA, BERKELEY

• • • • • • • •

THERE ARE TIMES YOU WANT TO STALK your professor, but beware! There's a fine line between eager and annoying. If you cross the line, your professor will try to avoid you. In freshman year I had a professor who I admired and wanted to learn from. A few times, I popped by his office—not even *looking* at his posted office hours! I soon got the hint that I should schedule something. If I ran into him, I'd mention that I'd like to make an appointment and he was very responsive. Remember, professors aren't always in their office for students. They may be working on research or engaged in something else, so don't assume they're there just for you at all times!

—A.S.
NEW YORK, NEW YORK
QUEEN'S UNIVERSITY

BEFORE I GOT INTO MY MAJOR, my professors in my core courses didn't know me from the man in the moon, even if I had two or more classes with them.

—NICOLE GREEN
CHICAGO, ILLINOIS

• • • • • • • •

DON'T BE AFRAID TO VOICE your opinion to a professor who does not know how to teach. There are too many professors who only teach because they have a degree. If they don't straighten up, go to the dean. Why pay top dollar for a course when the only thing you will remember about it is that fact that you didn't want to go?

—ZAKIA SIPP
CHICAGO, ILLINOIS
CHICAGO STATE UNIVERSITY

PRACTICE TALKING TO YOUR PROFESSORS

As an advisor, I often help my students "practice" for meetings with professors. I ask them questions that may come up, and help them prepare topics for discussion. If you have an advisor who can do this with you, don't be too shy to take advantage of the opportunity.

I'VE BECOME FRIENDS WITH ONE of my professors and sometimes we go to lunch together. I now consider him both my mentor and a friend. I want to go to law school when I graduate, so he has been advising me on which courses to take, what to read, and when to start preparing for the LSAT. I feel really lucky, since I am from a foreign country and it would have been really hard for me to figure everything out on my own.

—F.T.
LOS ANGELES, CALIFORNIA
UNIVERSITY OF CALIFORNIA, LOS ANGELES

• • • • • • • • •

Don't always agree with your professors, and voice your views openly. Good professors are open to conflicting opinions.

—D.N.M.
SEATTLE,
WASHINGTON
WASHINGTON
UNIVERSITY IN
ST. LOUIS

IT'S GREAT TO KNOW YOUR PROFESSORS outside of class. I went to one professor to try to get a research opportunity for the summer. She liked me from the initial interview. Later on, when I applied for a committee that she is in charge of, having had that research position with her increased my chances of getting in. She'll be writing me a recommendation to study abroad next year, and I'll probably be asking her for a recommendation for graduate school.

—ANONYMOUS
HOLMDEL, NEW JERSEY
CALIFORNIA INSTITUTE OF TECHNOLOGY

A STAR TEACHER

The professors I respected most and learned the most from were those who had spent much of their careers working in the field and then took up teaching. They had so much knowledge to impart. They were also the most passionate about their teaching and the subjects they taught. Professor Cronin was a probation officer by day and a college professor by night. She started her career as a social worker but found she really enjoyed working with troubled youth so she went into juvenile probation. I always enjoyed taking her classes, not because they were easy—she was one of the toughest teachers in the program—but because she was such a wonderful teacher. She had examples and stories for everything. Because she had been there and seen this stuff, she knew what she was talking about. Professor Cronin not only did her best to teach us in the classroom, she also went out of her way get us out in the field, from ride-alongs with police and probation officers to field trips to prisons. She'd bring someone she knew—other experts in the field, such as psychologists, police officers, or social workers—into class to speak to us. Professor Cronin was one of my favorite teachers.

—J.B.
RIVERSIDE, CALIFORNIA
CALIFORNIA STATE UNIVERSITY, SAN BERNARDINO

I TOOK TWO OR THREE CLASSES with my advisor, a religion professor. He'd spent a lot of time in India and was very dynamic in the classroom—he'd wave his hands about and make funny faces. We just appreciated each other. I went in for mandatory advising sessions and started asking about his trips to India and how he got to be a professor. He was happy to talk about it. Making the effort to go see a professor during his or her office hours is totally worthwhile. I ended up being good friends with him.

—H.D.
WESTIN, CONNECTICUT
SWARTHMORE COLLEGE

Go to their office hours. It's amazing what a little face time can do when it comes to your semester grades.

—*RICK HURCKES*
CHICAGO, ILLINOIS
UNIVERSITY OF DENVER

SOMETIMES YOU COME ACROSS a professor who doesn't encourage you to pursue your goals. Don't pay attention; go for it. I spoke to one of my sociology professors about my intent to write a book and he told me that I couldn't write a book and that it takes years and years of experience and research to write a book. He essentially said that I was too naive to take on something like that. I was so insulted. I pushed forward, though, and ended up completing original research for a thesis.

—JASON SIEGEL
BERKELEY, CALIFORNIA
UNIVERSITY OF CALIFORNIA, BERKELEY GPA: 3.85

THREE WAYS TO MAKE A GREAT FIRST IMPRESSION AT OFFICE HOURS

1. Shake hands and introduce yourself—tell the professor your name, your year, and what class you are taking.
2. Prepare a few questions in advance that show you have done the reading and thought about the course topics.
3. When you leave, thank the professor for talking with you. A little courtesy goes a long way!

TAKE PROFESSORS UP ON THEIR OFFERS of help. If they tell you they are willing to look over a paper or a project before the due date, take advantage of that. It's like getting a "do-over" in case you didn't do it right the first time. It can also make a difference in your grade. Several times I have taken papers to my professors for their review and have been told that what I have will receive a B. With their feedback, I was able to make changes and receive an A.

—NATALEE
MARTINS FERRY, OHIO
XAVIER UNIVERSITY

NEED ANOTHER REASON TO GO TO OFFICE HOURS?

Many academic departments and programs have scholarships to offer. Sometimes, the selection process consists simply of faculty sitting around a table and coming up with names of deserving students. If your professors know you and your work and think well of you, an unexpected bonus could come your way.

I HAVE A PROFESSOR THAT I often say hello to in my journalism major. He was the former vice president of the Associated Press. He has so many connections. One semester, I was doing a term paper and I went to him and said, "Hey, I really need to talk to someone at the *Wall Street Journal* for this term paper. But I'm just hitting dead ends." He said, "I've got some good friends up there. Why don't I give you their personal numbers and cell phone numbers?" He didn't have to help me out that much, but he did because he knew me.

—ELEANOR W. HAND
ATLANTA, GEORGIA
UNIVERSITY OF GEORGIA

I FELT TOO INTIMIDATED TO TALK to my professors in a lecture class. I just thought my question wouldn't seem urgent, so I stayed away. However, when the class size got smaller and my self-esteem grew, I would tell my professors if I was having problems. One music professor gave me worksheets he made up himself along with a packet to help me study. After, he would call my name after class to come see him, just to make sure I was on top of things.

—CHANA SERGEANT
CHICAGO, ILLINOIS
NORTHERN ILLINOIS UNIVERSITY

One professor was a great mentor to me. He connected me with various people within the department for some extracurricular activities, which not only provided me with hands-on experience, but helped boost my GPA.

—ANONYMOUS
NEW YORK, NEW YORK

THE SCHOLARLY MINDSET

Many professors are introverts. If they weren't, they would have trouble spending months and years researching and pondering their scholarly specialties. This personality trait can sometimes make communicating with your professor a bit challenging. His or her mind may be focused on a new archaeological discovery when you just want to ask for an extension on Monday's paper. Also, you've probably heard of the "absent-minded professor" stereotype—but how about the cranky, over-committed, flaky, or anti-social professor?

Most professors really do like students, but it doesn't always look that way. In addition, some of your professors are awfully busy. Some are teaching so many sections, they are constantly racing from one place to another. They may want to chat with you but just don't have a minute to spare. Others, particularly those trying to earn tenure, are under enormous pressure to get books and articles published and win acclaim in their field. Of course, there are also some professors who are just rude. Fortunately, they are the minority.

Don't be put off by one bad experience talking to a professor. He might have been in a hurry; she might have been preoccupied with the fate of the paper she submitted to *The Journal of Positive Social Psychology*. If you want to connect, seek out your professor when he or she is at relative leisure.

E-MAIL ETIQUETTE

Here are some do's and don'ts for communicating with faculty and staff:

DO	DON'T
• Use your college e-mail account.	• Use an informal (personal) e-mail account for a formal message.
• Use an informative, appropriate subject.	• Leave the subject line blank, or fill it with fluff (like "how's it goin'?").
• Use correct, standard English.	• Use abbreviations, emoticons, ALL CAPITALS, or all lowercase letters.
• Start with pleasantries.	• Forget your manners.
• Be concise and get to the point.	• Leave your reader confused as to why you're writing.
• Use the active tense ("I'm sorry I missed class.").	• Use the passive tense ("It was not possible for me to show up.").
• Call people by the names/titles they prefer.	• Ignore cues about how people like to be addressed.
• Read over your message and fix any mistakes.	• Be in too much of a hurry, and send a flawed message.
• Use e-mail for appropriate purposes.	• Use e-mail for very sensitive matters. Talk in person or use the phone.

SIMILE CORNER

A professor is like a doctor; he or she is a professional with many years of training and a wealth of expert knowledge—and like a patient, you are the one who is ultimately responsible for seeking out the health care (read: education) you need. Advisors like to use this simile, which dates back to Daniel Coit Gilman, who was President of Johns Hopkins University in 1886 when he declared, "The advisor's relation to the student is like that of a lawyer to his client or of a physician to one who seeks his counsel."

I'VE FOUND THAT NO MATTER how crazy the professor may seem; asking for help if I'm confused is always better than pretending to know in class and then asking others. If you see the professor and still need help, get it from classmates or the tutoring center. But letting the professor know you're stumbling but trying gets you an extra bit of understanding that you won't get otherwise!

—S.B.
SOUTH BEND, INDIANA
BALL STATE UNIVERSITY

Making the Grade (or Not): Failure, Stress & Coping

As you read this chapter, you will hear stories from many students who were in real jeopardy at one time or another, and managed to cope in many different ways. All those coping strategies have one thing in common: action. Nobody in this chapter bounced back from failure or overcame their stress and anxiety by sitting around and thinking, "I'll wait and see what happens … I hope some deus ex machina will sort out my problem … My way of doing things hasn't worked in the past, but maybe this time will be different … " These students took charge. Their stories prove that adversity doesn't define us; how we respond to adversity does.

One coping strategy that appears again and again in this chapter is stepping back from your schoolwork to clear your mind, returning to it calmer, refreshed, and motivated. I use this strategy in my own life. I have both a macro- and a micro version. The micro version comes into play when I'm doing a lengthy reading assignment. I give myself little breaks between sections to make tea or tidy my apartment. Believe it or not, these are activities I enjoy a lot, especially compared to some of my really dry readings. For the macro version, I'll go for a long walk along the Hudson River, read a mystery novel, or take the time to cook one of my favorite foods from scratch. All these activities help me relax and remember who I am—and part of who I am is a graduate student who cares deeply about doing well in her studies.

Read on to hear about what other students do. You will recognize some kindred spirits.

I WAS DOING HORRIBLY in a really hard chemistry class and I was freaking out about it. I ended up dropping the course a third of the way through and retaking it the next semester, when I made an A. Sometimes you can't handle certain hard classes in the midst of a really heavy semester or you may have a really tough professor.

—A.C.C.
AUSTIN, TEXAS
UNIVERSITY OF TEXAS AT AUSTIN GPA: 3.8

. . . .

THE SECOND SEMESTER of my junior year I decided out of the blue that I was interested in advertising. I took an advertising course, and I didn't do that well—I think I got a C. But I don't regret it. Even though I did get a bad grade, it's as important to eliminate possibilities as it is to get an idea of what you want to do.

—A.K.
POUND RIDGE, NEW YORK
BOSTON COLLEGE

. . . .

I FLUNKED A GEOMETRY COURSE my freshman year. The professor and the study groups did their best, but I didn't know it well in high school so I didn't expect to get it in college. But I didn't have a tantrum, like some students. It would take way more than an F to discourage me. I just took it over again, got a C, and life goes on.

Consider

—BETH HARVEY
CHICAGO, ILLINOIS
KENTUCKY WESLEYAN COLLEGE

WORST STUDY MISTAKE

THE BIGGEST MISTAKE I made during my freshman year was reading everything that was assigned. In my biology class I read every word from the book. When it came time for finals I was overwhelmed by how much information was *not* on the exam, and I was confused by all the information I had in my head. After that I only used my books as supplemental to what the professor taught in class. Don't over-read for your classes; it will only mess you up.

—NOEL
VANCOUVER, CANADA
UNIVERSITY OF SOUTHERN CALIFORNIA GPA: 3.72

• • • • • • • • •

THE WORST THING YOU CAN DO is to look at the first few problems of your homework and assume because you know the first few sets that you'll know everything and ace the test. You won't. Put yourself in a testing environment and attempt to do a problem. Do it without your notes and without external help. It's really easy to convince yourself that you know something when you really don't. When you are in a test environment and you are crunched for time, everything is completely different.

—NATHANIEL
PHILADELPHIA, PENNSYLVANIA
STANFORD UNIVERSITY GPA: 3.7

ON THE FIRST DAY OF CLASS, the professor told everyone that there were going to be three tests, and she would drop the test with the lowest score to calculate our final grade. I just assumed that I could skip one of the tests entirely, so I just didn't show up to take the second test. This was probably the worst mistake I made in my four years in school. The professor ended up giving me a zero and explained that she meant us to take all three tests. Even if I failed one, I was still supposed to show up. It was awful because I got A's on the other two tests, but only ended up with a C in the class.

—BRETT
FT. LEE, NEW JERSEY
PENNSYLVANIA STATE UNIVERSITY

. . . .

THE WORST PRESENTATION I ever gave was in an international relations class. I lost my voice the night before and couldn't say a word when I got up in front of the class to present. I was so upset since I'd spent weeks preparing and knew I would get an A. Fortunately the professor excused me and offered me extra credit to do, instead of the presentation.

—ANONYMOUS
SEATTLE, WASHINGTON
NEW YORK UNIVERSITY GPA: 3.72

MY BIGGEST STUDY MISTAKE was not going to class and thinking I could study everything on my own by reading the textbook. In class you can take all the notes and go back over them later. It really helps to have those notes. Since I had already taken a few computer science classes I thought I could start staying home from subsequent classes while doing the reading on my own. It never worked. For a while I thought I was getting something done, but when I took my midterm I failed completely.

—NANA KOFI KORANTENG OHENE-ADU
ACCRA, GHANA
STANFORD UNIVERSITY

• • • • • • • • •

IN A FRESHMAN ENGLISH CLASS, I read the wrong book for a class discussion that was part of my grade. I read a book that we were going to be tested on later in the semester. When I got to class the day of the discussion, I had so much confidence until the professor asked someone a question about a character I had never heard of. Before my turn to answer came, I realized the mistake I had made. I left the class and took a zero on the assignment.

—J.A.
BOSTON, MASSACHUSETTS
UNIVERSITY OF SOUTHERN CALIFORNIA GPA: 3.8

EVEN A D- ISN'T THE END of the world. That's the grade I ended up with when I took Ancient Greek in my second year. It obviously affected my grade point average, but I did get the credit for it and I still have a 3.5.

—MICHELLE WADDELL
HOLLYWOOD, FLORIDA
WASHINGTON UNIVERSITY IN ST. LOUIS GPA: 3.38

I flunked out. It was too much freedom: Nobody but your conscience telling you when to go to bed, when to study, who to date, and what to wear. I lost control.

—MARIJOSEPHE PIERRE
PLANO, ILLINOIS
ELMHURST COLLEGE

I TOLD MY NEIGHBORS when they left for college to study very hard their freshman year because one poor grade can drag down your grade point average. I received a D in one class my junior year and, despite good grades in all of my other classes, it kept me from graduating with honors.

—MICHELE
ROCKAWAY TOWNSHIP, NEW JERSEY
BOSTON UNIVERSITY

I HAD A CLOSE FRIEND who failed a couple of freshman classes. It seems that freshmen commonly fail because they take their classes for granted and don't understand the commitment of college. My friend disliked his college and tried to make his experience better by increasing the fun. It's the late partying and such that sidetrack you and essentially break you. Failing is a wake-up call. All that money wasted because I preferred Hamm's to my books. It's all about priorities and independence. It's the true test. It's not, "Can I live independently from my parents and handle my responsibilities?" It's "Can I succeed on my own?"

—LAURA GLASS
GOLDEN VALLEY, MINNESOTA
UNIVERSITY OF ST. THOMAS

• • • • • • • • •

DURING THE FIRST PART of my freshman year, parties and football games took precedence over studying, and I spent the second semester on probation. It all became very depressing, and I ended up leaving school at the end of year one. Many years later, when I returned to complete my undergraduate degree, I made the Dean's List and ultimately graduated with honors. I went on to pursue a master's degree in social work, ending my college education with a nearly perfect GPA.

—CINDY
ST. LOUIS, MISSOURI
WASHINGTON UNIVERSITY IN ST. LOUIS

A VALUABLE LESSON INDEED

I really hated my freshman math class because it was boring and it was at the end of a long day day. At the end of one class, a few students asked the professor if it was necessary to come to the class. The professor told them that it was not and that they could just follow the syllabus and come to class for exams. I thought that was a good idea and believed that I could teach myself the work. I basically stopped going to class and put my time to better use; I went to the movies and the guitar center. Anyway, I showed up for class on exam day and class was going on as usual and my professor was not handing out exams. I thought it was strange and when I asked the professor about it, she said that everyone was doing so well in the class so she decided to give the exam a week earlier. I missed the exam and ended up failing the class and I had to take it all over again. This taught me a very valuable lesson.

—MATT BOWEN
BALTIMORE, MARYLAND
UNIVERSITY OF MARYLAND

THE WAY I MADE GOOD GRADES was that I chose not to have fun until my junior year. Freshman and sophomore year, I pretended that the study lounge was the club and the books were cute guys who wanted to get to know me, so I didn't get bored.

> —ANONYMOUS
> CHICAGO, ILLINOIS
> SOUTHERN ILLINOIS UNIVERSITY, CARBONDALE

* * * * * * * * *

UCSD HAS A CULTURAL DIVERSITY requirement and I thought sign language would be the least painful of all of the choices, so I took it. It turned out to be harder than I thought and because it was hard for me to learn, I hated it. I ended up getting a C+ in it, and I never get low grades.

> —MARIA ROMANO
> SAN DIEGO, CALIFORNIA
> UNIVERSITY OF CALIFORNIA, SAN DIEGO

* * * * * * * * *

DON'T STRESS OUT SO MUCH about your studies. There is a lot of grade inflation here, so you could end up studying really hard and not get an A, or study half as much and get an A- or B. The amount you have to study to get an A is disproportionate to the amount you need to study to get a B+. I think you come out ahead if you study less.

> —MARIA
> MORAGO, CALIFORNIA
> STANFORD UNIVERSITY

TO RELIEVE STRESS, I love to read. And not just serious books, but something like the newspaper. I like sports and I love reading *Sports Illustrated*. I'm also in the band and I go to all the football games. The old saying goes, "All work and no play makes Jack a dull boy." Plus, you'll burn out. So get into something. The sporting events are pretty fun.

—NED
NEW ORLEANS, LOUISIANA
YALE UNIVERSITY

. . . .

I DO A LOT OF SERVICE WORK. That is a huge stress reducer. You go out on field trips on Saturday morning with friends, and you're also getting exercise from the work you are doing. It's also psychologically beneficial because you know that you're helping people and making a difference.

—JON WALDO
NASHVILLE, TENNESSEE
BOSTON UNIVERSITY

. . . .

IN MY SENIOR YEAR, every Friday a group of us would find very cheap tickets to a symphony or opera. It was nice to know that at the end of the week, you can relax, even sleep!

—REBECCA
MOORESTOWN, NEW JERSEY
WASHINGTON UNIVERSITY

Lots of college students like to drink to blow off stress, but if you have something important to do the next day, that could be tragic.

—KRISTEN
DOBBINS
ORLAND PARK,
ILLINOIS
UNIVERSITY
OF WISCONSIN

OVERCOMING PROCRASTINATION

When I taught a course called Developing Academic Success, my students identified procrastination as their number one obstacle. Procrastination is so prevalent that scientists are beginning to study it. I don't have a cure, but I do have one tip, and it is drawn from physics.

We know that a body at rest tends to remain at rest, and a body in motion tends to remain in motion. Sir Isaac Newton might also have told us that a body that is studying tends to keep studying. Here's proof:

The very act of avoiding our work takes an enormous amount of energy. Think of all the stress you experience when you know you need to sit down and read your chemistry textbook, but you continue to put it off all week. You never feel quite easy in your mind because you know, come exam day, your procrastination will have dire consequences. You may use the time that you steal from your academics to do something fun, but you don't enjoy yourself as much.

Now think of how much energy it will cost you to sit down and work just for five minutes. Hardly any, right? But when you begin studying, that guilty feeling drops away and is replaced by a burst of virtuous energy. Working actually takes less energy than worrying about not working!

GETTING A B WAS LIKE AN F to me. And that's what my statistics professor gave me my third year in college. Somehow he found out my record, and kept mocking me by telling me his class would be the hardest ever. He would challenge anything I said. So, he gave me a B. I went to the dean about it, but the next semester the professor was gone. I still got stuck with the B, but at least I knew another straight A student wouldn't become a victim.

—EVENS ALEXIS
CALUMET CITY, ILLINOIS
CHICAGO STATE UNIVERSITY

• • • • • • • •

I PLAY INTER-HOUSE SPORTS to help me relieve stress and get my mind off work. We have eight resident houses, and the different houses compete against each other. It's all for fun: there are scheduled games and you can choose the ones you want to play.

—DANIEL
MARLTON, NEW JERSEY
CALIFORNIA INSTITUTE OF TECHNOLOGY

• • • • • • • •

WE HAD AN "ABS OF STEEL" videotape (also "Buns of Steel" and "Thighs of Steel"). They were five-minute workouts that we would squeeze in when we felt like we needed a break from studying or wanted to procrastinate. We would curse at the instructor on the tape.

—NINA
SAN FRANCISCO, CALIFORNIA
UNIVERSITY OF WASHINGTON GPA: 3.4

When I get extremely stressed out or need a break from studying I usually end up going shopping for an hour or two, just to clear my mind.

*—RACHEL
ALDRICH
BROOKLYN
PARK,
MINNESOTA
UNIVERSITY
OF WISCONSIN
GPA: 3.7*

MY FRESHMAN YEAR I was studying for an economics exam, a notoriously stressful experience. Since there were several classes all taking the same course, there were a lot of people studying for the same exam. That's a lot of collective stress. Around midnight the de-stress valve known as the "econ scream" opened up. First, I heard one scream from outside the window, then another. Soon, the quad was filled with shouts of students sticking their heads out of their dorm windows to scream. Somehow, hearing all those screams relaxed me, and made me feel like I wasn't alone.

—DANIEL
NEW YORK, NEW YORK
UNIVERSITY OF PENNSYLVANIA GPA: 3.7

• • • • • • • •

As corny as it is, the best advice I ever received is to never give up. I had a hard freshman year, but because of professors who never gave up on me, I have succeeded since then.

—JENNA PAIGE SWEENEY
RICHARDSON, TEXAS
BAYLOR UNIVERSITY GPA: 3.5

FUN FACTS ABOUT COLLEGE-THEMED TV SHOWS

Felicity (1998-2002)
Felicity is in love with classmate Ben. Since she works in the admissions office, she decides to read his file and even photocopy part of his application, later talking to him about it. So inappropriate!

Beverly Hills 90210 (Seasons 4 through 7)
Brandon, Kelly, Donna, David, and Steve graduated from high school and went to college at the same time I did. Use your college-honed math skills to figure out how old I am!

Dawson's Creek (Seasons 5 & 6)
Joey Potter goes to see her grades posted on the wall outside the registrar's office. Grades cannot be posted in that way because it is a violation of the Family Educational Rights and Privacy Act.

Tommy Lee Goes to College (2005)
You have to appreciate Tommy Lee's enthusiastic use of college resources such as tutoring. This show also reminds us that higher education welcomes the "non-traditional" student.

ADDICTED TO THE DRAMA?

Years ago, my college roommate and I were very concerned about a friend of ours. She seemed to have so much on her plate and appeared to be on the verge of some kind of breakdown. We soon realized, however, that our friend *always* seemed that way. It wasn't an exception for her; it was the rule. We loved our friend as much as ever, but we decided to stop worrying, because she clearly enjoyed her panicked state. We stopped offering help and advice after learning that she didn't want to change the situation as much as she wanted to tell us about it, at great length and with great passion.

Are you a drama addict too? See if you answer "yes" to any of the following questions.

- When things are kind of slow, do you pick fights with your loved ones to get things going again?
- After a fight, do you find yourself going back "just to say one more thing"?
- Do you wait until the last minute to start a paper because you "can only work under pressure"?
- Do you feel empty and unfulfilled if you aren't committed to more courses and activities than anyone on your hall?

- Do you enjoy impressing (or trying to impress) faculty and staff with how many clubs you run, how many hours you work, and how many credits you're taking?

Even if you answered "yes" to *all* of the questions, you might not have a problem. If you're getting everything done to your satisfaction, you're maintaining good health, and your friends still like you, don't worry about it.

But if any of these areas of your life are suffering due to your speed-of-light lifestyle, it's time to take a *slow* walk over to see a resident advisor, academic advisor, or counselor.

I ALWAYS FEEL STRESSED OUT around exam time. I work full time and, unfortunately, my job always tends to get busier around finals. I've come to the understanding that I can only do so much and that overwhelming myself with all the tasks I have to complete is self-defeating. Now, I schedule my time carefully and give myself periodic milestones as opposed to trying to accomplish everything all at once. This way I know I'm making progress and my workload is not a constant source of stress.

—TARA
ARLINGTON, VIRGINIA
DUKE UNIVERSITY

• • • • • • • •

WORKING OUT KEEPS you motivated and gives you energy to work hard to get that A. I spend a lot of my time at the gym and that helps me focus. When I'm working out I reflect on my day's worth of class. It also cleans my body out so I can stay alert.

—A.L.
HILLSBOROUGH, CALIFORNIA
UNIVERSITY OF CALIFORNIA, DAVIS GPA: 3.65

• • • • • • • •

I GO TO THE GYM FIVE TO SIX DAYS a week. If I don't do that I will sit there in my dorm and do nothing. Exercise is a great break. I get tired after 45 minutes and I want to go home, and then I can study.

—ANNA
PRINCETON, NEW JERSEY
PRINCETON UNIVERSITY

THE WEEKLY AFTERNOON PARTIES one semester kept me from having a nervous breakdown. The parties were called "sock hops." We would go into one of the assigned rooms on campus and take off our shoes and start dancing, hopping, kicking, and stepping with the boys like it was midnight. I would feel like I was back in high school again with no worries.

—YVETTE DAVIS
CHICAGO, ILLINOIS
UNIVERSITY OF ILLINOIS GPA: 2.8

. . . .

I BLOW OFF STRESS WITH A GOOD RUN. I get out for anywhere from a half hour to a whole hour and sweat it all out. It clears my mind and gets everything moving again.

—KERRY COOLEY
LONG LAKE, MINNESOTA
VILLANOVA UNIVERSITY

. . . .

I FAILED CALCULUS THE FIRST TIME I took it. I didn't like the professor, I didn't like the TA, so I just stopped going. I ended up dropping it and took an F in the class, but I knew that I could take it over and my new grade would replace the F. The second time I took it, I ended up getting an A. I think I was more mature the second time around, and I got a lot of help and support from my friends who had already taken it and done well.

—LINDA SIN
PASADENA, CALIFORNIA
UNIVERSITY OF CALIFORNIA, BERKELEY

The best way to relieve stress during final exams and midterms is to spend time with your friends on study breaks— and laugh a lot.

—W.L.H.
WASHINGTON, D.C.
DUKE UNIVERSITY

COLLEGE SCHEDULES CAN GET really stressful. Sometimes I go to bed a little earlier and I'll wake up early—at 7:30 in the morning—and I'll go have a nice breakfast and have some time to think. That really helps.

—RIDA
REDERACH, PENNSYLVANIA
BOSTON UNIVERSITY

· · · · · · · ·

WHENEVER I GOT STRESSED, I would just go home. That was the beauty of living only 45 minutes away from school. Plus, my mom went to my college part-time to get her master's degree, so I would see her twice a week. We would have a girls' day out at the mall and dinner. That always put a band-aid on my gunshot wounds.

—JAMAE TERRY
ST. LOUIS, MISSOURI
SOUTHERN ILLINOIS UNIVERSITY, CARBONDALE

· · · · · · · ·

I GOT INTO CYCLING MY SOPHOMORE YEAR. I would bike six to seven days a week, in the afternoons or evenings. Toward the end of the semester, course workload would get too busy. But I noticed that I felt better and it actually made studying a little bit easier. As far as time management goes, things that feel like a waste of time can actually help you in the long run, even though you're not reading a book or studying.

—JASON BRUNER
CARTERSVILLE, GEORGIA
GARDNER-WEBB UNIVERSITY

GOING OUT IS A STRESS REDUCER for me. I find it easier to focus if I go out. For me, if I work all day for a week straight, I get really anxious and I have a lot of excess energy. And sports don't expel that energy: partying is the only way to do that.

—MERRITT
CHICAGO, ILLINOIS
PRINCETON UNIVERSITY

Every Wednesday night from 10 p.m. until midnight, I spend that time in an improv group where I can just release everything and have a good time.

—ROB MCLEMORE
ST. LOUIS, MISSOURI

THERE WERE TIMES WHEN I just felt overwhelmed and completely stressed. There were days I'd skip classes for the day and totally unwind. I'd feel refreshed enough to do my work and be totally prepared for the next day. It probably happened once a semester.

—ELIZABETH
MOORESTOWN, NEW JERSEY
FAIRFIELD UNIVERSITY

A COUPLE OF MONTHS INTO my first semester, I realized partying was not worth damaging a possible 4.0 GPA. I found out I was partying with the same people over and over again—same old faces and conversations, just different venue. I was saying to myself, "These are the same people I saw at the party last week, and I'm going to see them in class tomorrow." Seeing people on my lunch breaks was good enough for me.

—SYREETA BURNETT
WHEATON, ILLINOIS
DEPAUL UNIVERSITY

• • • • • • • •

IT'S REALLY IMPORTANT TO DISENGAGE yourself once in a while from whatever you are regularly involved with. I played sports in high school and thought that was the pinnacle of my sports career since I wasn't going to play any varsity sport at Berkeley. But then I discovered a whole new world of intramural sports. I play about twice a week and it helps a lot. Playing sports relieves stress and it allows you to meet new people. On any given day I can be hanging out on campus, kicking around a soccer ball, and the next thing I know I'm involved in a ten-on-ten soccer game.

—EDWARD WEAVERLING
BERKELEY, CALIFORNIA
UNIVERSITY OF CALIFORNIA, BERKELEY

Through the Lean Times: Support Services & Staying Motivated

In this chapter, Jodie from Indiana says that you might as well take advantage of your college's support services since they're free. Well—sort of. You are paying for them through your tuition and fees, which is all the more reason to go.

And there's no reason to feel embarrassed when you visit a support services office. They wouldn't exist if students didn't need them. In fact, when you go, you are not just helping yourself; you may be helping the office survive. Some support services are required to justify their funding every year or so by reporting on how many students they have served. More students coming through the doors means the doors will stay open.

What can you expect from the support services on your campus? Sometimes all you need is an answer to a sticky grammar problem, or a note excusing you from classes for a few days to take care of a short-term family situation. In other cases, expect (and be open to) more than just a quick fix. You can learn skills, whether academic or personal, that you'll use for a long time. Some support staff will (figuratively) walk along with you, helping you make plans and carry them out. Those plans could include getting off probation, getting onto the Dean's List, choosing a major, applying to graduate school—even coping with a personal tragedy. The administrators of your college have anticipated that all these things, and more, can take place in the lives of their students, and have developed support services accordingly.

Ultimately, a college cannot be successful unless its students are successful. Your college keeps track of how many students are able to stay in school, achieve honors, and get into graduate school or find excellent jobs. Support service professionals want all the good things for you that you want for yourself. So what are you waiting for?

MY COLLEGE OFFERS FREE TUTORING to students. I am a tutor for the freshman- and sophomore-level physics classes. I have seven students right now, so I tutor a lot. The students I help are allowed to see me as often as they want. The hours are very flexible so that more people will ask for help when they need it. They just come into my room whenever they have questions.

—LEYAN LO
BASKING RIDGE, NEW JERSEY
CALIFORNIA INSTITUTE OF TECHNOLOGY GPA: 3.7

. . . .

IN MY ENGLISH 101 CLASS, my professor made it mandatory for the class to see a writing coach. And we had to bring proof of their signatures and edits on our papers and discuss with the class the good writing tips we learned. And if we didn't incorporate that into our next papers, we got points taken off.

—KENDRA GONZALEZ
SCHAUMBURG, ILLINOIS
UNIVERSITY OF ILLINOIS

. . . .

I PUT A HEAVIER EMPHASIS than most on sleep. I had one of those episodes in the first semester when I did three all-nighters all in a row. I could hardly think straight. Today I had one hour less sleep than I usually do, and there was a big difference in my class: I had less focus and I was drowsy.

—JON WALDO
NASHVILLE, TENNESSEE
BOSTON UNIVERSITY

MY SCHOOL OFFERS MANY support services. I've used the career center, which has workshops around campus. They teach everything from taking good notes, to writing papers. The school also makes a lot of accommodations for students with disabilities. I have a few friends here who are disabled and they get a lot of help through support services. They get to make special arrangements with their professors to turn in papers later and to get things done in a manner that works for them.

—DANNY J. HERRERA
LYNWOOD, CALIFORNIA
UNIVERSITY OF CALIFORNIA, BERKELEY

• • • • • • • • •

Consider

IN MY FRESHMAN YEAR I went through a real problem with depression. My boyfriend broke up with me, my dad was sick, and I could *not* concentrate. I went to the counseling service on campus. They let me see a therapist, no charge. Actually, I couldn't relate at all to the first one (a middle-aged guy), and so then I got a younger woman. This helped me a lot, plus she had advice on what to tell my teachers. She knew some of them, too, so she kind of knew what would work with each one. Some teachers will give you as much leeway as they can, and some insist on a note from the counselor. I was very surprised at how much they worked with me so I could keep up my grades. I got past it all and am doing very well now.

—J.B.
JACKSON, MICHIGAN
UNIVERSITY OF MICHIGAN GPA: 3.5

A TURNING POINT

If you are not doing well in school stop blaming every-one else. You can only blame yourself for your own mis-takes. I was too lazy during the first two years of college. I partied all of the time and I just didn't study. During my second year, I read a book about how losers blame the outside world and blame everyone but themselves for their loss. I read it and I was like, "I don't want to be a loser." It was true; I blamed everyone but myself for the fact that I wasn't getting good grades in school. That was a real turning point for me. I started to study and I got A's all the way through graduation. Now I am at UC Berkeley getting my Masters in Journalism, so it was all worth it.

—OMAR FEKEIKI
BERKELEY, CALIFORNIA
ALTURATH UNIVERSITY COLLEGE, BAGHDAD

THERE ARE A LOT OF BUILT-IN support systems through my college's housing structure and there are upperclass counselors looking out for you all of the time here. They are there to provide unlimited counseling services and they can refer you to other places to get support when you need it.

—ANONYMOUS
SAN DIEGO, CALIFORNIA
CALIFORNIA INSTITUTE OF TECHNOLOGY

* * * * * * * *

Use tutors for more than just raising your GPA. I go to a Spanish tutor not to help me make a better grade, but to improve my Spanish-speaking skills.

—D.N.M.
SEATTLE, WASHINGTON
WASHINGTON UNIVERSITY IN ST. LOUIS

* * * * * * * *

TAKE ADVANTAGE OF SCHOOL BREAKS and social events. Also, become involved in something that is not related to academics. This helps to break up the monotony of schoolwork.

—LEIGH
CHICAGO, ILLINOIS
WESLEYAN UNIVERSITY

HELP DURING HARD TIMES

My dad died in March of my freshman year and I missed school for almost two weeks. When I got back, I had four tests, five papers, and a bunch of other assignments. I was really depressed and overwhelmed and didn't feel like doing anything—not even going to class. My mom convinced me to go to the health center and get some depression and anxiety medication, which I only took for a couple of weeks because I don't like to take medication for my problems. Then, I remembered a guy from the counseling center had come to my dorm room after my dad died, and I still had his card in my purse. I thought no one could really help me feel better, but I called the center anyway, and set up an appointment. I started seeing him a couple of times a week and he knew exactly what to say to me to make me feel better. "Tackle one thing at a time; professors will understand," he told me. If it weren't for him, I don't think I would have been able to finish the semester or return the next year.

—LIZ HAINES
KIRKSVILLE, MISSOURI
TRUMAN STATE UNIVERSITY

Consider

TO STAY MOTIVATED, I made sure that I had extracurricular activities so my life didn't solely focus on school. I was the wrestling manager for a while. I went to social events on campus, and hung out in other peoples' dorm rooms. I joined organizations so that I could meet people who shared my interests. I went on hiking trips and to downtown D.C.

—MELISSA BARBAGALLO DAVIS
BALTIMORE, MARYLAND
UNIVERSITY OF MARYLAND

• • • • • • • •

IF YOU ARE HAVING TROUBLE, ask for help. I have asked professors for help if I didn't understand something. It did help me understand the material better. I have also used a tutor for math, and it did help me get through the class, but I will never like math! These services are free, so take advantage of them.

—JODIE PIETRUCHA
MISHAWAKA, INDIANA
INDIANA UNIVERSITY, SOUTH BEND

• • • • • • • •

I WAS SO DETERMINED TO GRADUATE that I did it in three years. I went to school all year around, summers and intermissions. I knew that if I chose to drop out I would have no leeway. My parents weren't rich, and they would refuse to take care of me if I decided school wasn't for me.

—TIOMBE EILAND
CHICAGO, ILLINOIS
LOYOLA UNIVERSITY

REFERRALS FOR SUPPORT SERVICES

If you're not achieving the grades you would like, or you want to sign up for some extra support *before* you need it, your college has many resources for you. Tutoring, college skills courses, workshops, mentor programs—there can be many, many options. Your college may even have support programs you can only get into by application, invitation, or nomination. So how do you choose the best services for your needs? And how can you be sure you're not missing something really helpful?

Your academic advisor can select a list of resources for you, and may even be able to point you toward individuals in different offices. "Karen in the Counseling Center has a lot of experience working with students who have Internet addictions." "Mike in Academic Support Services has helped many of my advisees who are dyslexic. Would you like to call from my phone to schedule an appointment?"

It's up to you to take the first step toward tapping into college resources, but your academic advisor can make the journey to the right resources much shorter.

ACCENTUATE THE POSITIVE*

Have you ever heard the song that tells you to "accentuate the positive"? Let's take a moment and think about the elements of your life that are already contributing to your success in college:

- Pick one place that you like to go to because it relaxes you, helps you work, etc. ...
- Pick one person who inspires and supports you ...
- Pick one object that you couldn't work without ...
- Pick one skill you have that helps you achieve ...
- Pick one dream you have that motivates you to keep going ...

Remember these gifts every day—they are strengths you can build on!

(*Harold Arlen, Johnny Mercer, 1944)

SOME OF THE ARTICLES that my professors have assigned are found online, and those can be downloaded and auto-summarized in Microsoft Word. The technique back-fired on me only once when Microsoft Word failed to include four key points of a reading assignment. When my professor asked me to name one of the four, I couldn't do it. However, using this technique has never affected my grade because I only use it when I'm not being tested on the material.

—JASON PAUL TORREANO
LOCKPORT, NEW YORK
STATE UNIVERSITY OF NEW YORK, BROCKPORT

• • • • • • • • •

FRATERNITIES AREN'T JUST A BUNCH of guys throwing parties. I belong to one and the guys here have helped me stay focused and they've helped me by providing a sort of roadmap through my classes. My mom was the first person to question my desire to join a fraternity. She's really traditional and had set ideas that fraternities were all about partying, so she was completely against my involvement at first. In the end, I wouldn't have done it if I felt that it would impose on my academic life. It's a networking tool. We have study sessions together and just having all the guys around, especially the older ones, helps me get a better sense of what I should be doing academically.

—ALEX
ORANGE COUNTY, CALIFORNIA
UNIVERSITY OF CALIFORNIA, BERKELEY GPA: 3.79

Taking classes you love inspires you to get an A because you enjoy studying for them.

—GLADYS CHRISTIAN CHICAGO, ILLINOIS
CHICAGO STATE UNIVERSITY GPA: 3.6

I AM THE THIRD GENERATION of my family to graduate from my university, and when times got hard, I would think of when my mother was in school. She was a single mother with two kids, and my brother was classified as mentally retarded, and she still made it. So I kept her graduation picture by my bed. I looked at it before I went to sleep, so I would wake up with confidence.

—NICOLE GREEN
CHICAGO, ILLINOIS
CHICAGO STATE UNIVERSITY

DON'T BE INTIMIDATED BY professors or TAs. I used to think I was bothering them, but one time my friend and I were having trouble with an engineering problem, and we got help from a TA. Then, I found out by talking with other students that they all had needed assistance with the same problem.

—THEA
ST. LOUIS, MISSOURI
WASHINGTON UNIVERSITY GPA: 3.68

EVERY TIME I SCORED A B or higher on a test or paper, I would treat myself to a nice dress or a semi-expensive dinner. When I would get that A or B, I would smile so hard: My classmates would think I was just happy for a good grade, but I would be happy about the dress I've been staring at in the mall for weeks.

—KANEDA IRVIN
CHICAGO, ILLINOIS
SOUTHERN ILLINOIS UNIVERSITY, CARBONDALE

SIMILE CORNER

At a professional conference, I heard an attendee compare academic advisors to AAA: "We can bring out our maps and help you draw a route for yourself, but you have to drive the car!" This means that you bear the ultimate responsibility for informing yourself about academic requirements and college policies; for following up on suggestions, referrals, and opportunities; for making a careful, informed choice of major; and for taking the necessary steps to earn the grades you want.

I CAME FROM A PUBLIC SCHOOL in Los Angeles County, so my technology skills were already obsolete when I got to Stanford; I didn't even have high-speed Internet, so seeing that was really eye-opening to me. Also, such skills as PowerPoint were necessary. I learned this the hard way during my freshman Spanish class when I was required to make a presentation. I knew all of the information and I stuck pictures and notes on a nicely decorated poster board. I felt completely confident about my prep for my presentation until I got to class and saw everyone else with laptops and PowerPoint presentations.

—ANONYMOUS
LOS ANGELES, CALIFORNIA
STANFORD UNIVERSITY

THE ART OF THE NAP

I REDISCOVERED NAPPING IN COLLEGE. I'd spend a free hour in my bunk bed back in my dorm, and that little catnap refreshed me *so* much. It's a good way to spend time.

—JACLYN YOUHANA
LIBERTY TOWNSHIP, OHIO

• • • • • • • •

OVER THE LAST WEEK I'VE WORKED really hard and I've been really tired so I've been napping. A couple of days ago I woke up from my nap and I felt so refreshed and was able to work continuously for the next three hours. I tried it again the other day and I got the same result.

—MANPREET
LOS ANGELES, CALIFORNIA
UNIVERSITY OF SOUTHERN CALIFORNIA GPA: 3.9

• • • • • • • •

RECIPE FOR A GOOD NAP when you're finished cramming for exams: Take a hot shower, drink a hot toddy (some hot tea with whiskey, or just hot tea if you don't drink alcohol), and put on your jammies. I certainly had some awesome naps when finals were over. I even put a Do Not Disturb sign on my dorm room door.

—MICHAEL PAOLI
NEW YORK, NEW YORK
UNIVERSITY OF TORONTO GPA: 3.4

MY BEST NAP EVER: After the fourth of my finals that were all in a row, I was walking home and it started pouring rain. I swear I almost cried. I finally got to my apartment and slept for over 10 hours.

—A.C.C.
AUSTIN, TEXAS
UNIVERSITY OF TEXAS AT AUSTIN GPA: 3.8

MY BEST NAP EVER HAPPENED the day after midterm finals. I had a three-hour train ride home to visit my family and I don't remember a thing from the trip! I think I even napped with a smile on my face because the weight of the exam was off my shoulders.

—A.S.
NEW YORK, NEW YORK
QUEEN'S UNIVERSITY

MY BEST NAP EVER WAS ON A FLIGHT home to Seattle right after I finished my last two exams. As soon as I finished my tests I drove to the airport, got on the plane, lay down, and closed my eyes. Five hours later, the flight attendant woke me up. I have no recollection of the flight; it felt like ten minutes to me.

—ANONYMOUS
SEATTLE, WASHINGTON
NEW YORK UNIVERSITY GPA: 3.7

THE BEST NAP I EVER TOOK was after an all-nighter. I just finished the exam that I'd been studying for and I walked outside, sat down under a tree, and slept there for two hours. I felt like a new person and when I woke up, the sky was crystal blue and the weather was perfect.

—J.A.
BOSTON, MASSACHUSETTS
UNIVERSITY OF SOUTHERN CALIFORNIA GPA: 3.8

• • • • • • • •

MY BEST NAP EVER OCCURRED when I found a couch that had been sitting near a window. The sun had been shining on it for a while, warming the seat. I just curled up like a cat on the couch, basking in the sun!

—BRITTANY
DALLAS, TEXAS
UNIVERSITY OF OKLAHOMA GPA: 4

• • • • • • • •

NAPS IN THE LIBRARY ARE A LIFESAVER, especially if you can snag a comfy chair. Just make sure you give yourself enough time to wake up and glance in a mirror before you take off to your next class. You don't want to be the kid with hair sticking up and a fabric impression on your face.

—MYSTI SKYE NIERMANN
CONROE, TEXAS
WASHINGTON UNIVERSITY IN ST. LOUIS GPA: 3.3

WORKING AT AN ON-CAMPUS dining hall was the smartest thing I ever did at college. Eating well is important if you want to stay focused on your schoolwork and other activities, and instant noodles or mac and cheese do not have nutritional value. Takeout is expensive and your parents can't freeze an entire semester's worth of their home cooking for you. While the job wasn't glamorous and the pay might not have been as good as other jobs on campus, I was well fed. And with the money I saved not buying food, I was able to buy more important things—like books.

—JACOB SZE
ELLENVILLE, NEW YORK
CORNELL UNIVERSITY

• • • • • • • •

When I start losing my motivation, I always remind myself that a break is a couple of months or weeks away. In the meantime, I make lists to get a sense of control over my work.

— AMANDA TUST
EAST STROUDSBURG, PENNSYLVANIA
UNIVERSITY OF SAN DIEGO

THE COLLEGE LIBRARY: SMART PEOPLE GO HERE

I went to a good college with an amazing library, but I barely used it until my senior year. I was too intimidated to explore on my own, and too embarrassed to ask for help. So I spent the next three years walking down the hill into town to use the public library, which looked a lot more like what I was used to. Just imagine how much better my papers would have been if I had used my college library; if I had studied in the quiet, peaceful library instead of the bustling pizza shop in the student center. My books usually smelled like pizza and I absorbed more pepperoni and less knowledge.

In my senior year, I applied for and was given a study carrel in the library. It was like heaven—a tiny room of my own on the top floor under a glass skylight. I used my study carrel while I was writing my senior thesis. I was in and out of the library so often then that I started to feel like I belonged. I found wonderful books for my research. I finally figured out how to use that computerized catalog. I found the circulation desk. By the time I graduated, I had come to love the library. If only I had been using it all along!

FUN FACTS ABOUT GRADUATION

- Graduation is sometimes referred to as "commence-ment," even though it takes place at the *end* of your college experience. This term comes from an ancient university tradition. Centuries ago, students who had finished their studies were then allowed to sit with the teachers at the "commensa," or common table.

- When it's time for you to graduate, you will purchase a cap and gown to wear for the ceremony, but in past centuries, many colleges expected students to wear their academic garb at all times! You could even get in trouble if you were caught going to class with-out it. A modified version of this tradition continues at Oxford University in England, where students today are expected to don their caps and gowns for certain college activities.

DON'T FORGET TO TAKE TIME for yourself. There's always more to do, and it will still be there after a short break. Schedule a little time each day to do something that is not school-related.

—A.F.
CINCINNATI, OHIO

ACADEMIC ADVISING: GETTING STARTED

The biggest myth about academic advising is that advising is all about course selection. There is so much more to it. If you are willing to put in the time and effort, a good academic advisor will help you discover your strengths, develop as a learner, clarify your life goals, and make a plan to accomplish your dreams.

Different colleges have vastly different academic advising systems. In some colleges, faculty members do all the advising. In others, professional staff (like me) fill this role. Still other colleges use a combination. Caseload methods also vary: are you assigned a specific academic advisor, or do you go to an advising center and see the first person available? To get the most out of whatever your college's advising model happens to be, check your student handbook, catalog, or college web site to figure out how it works. You can also ask your RA or orientation counselor.

Then see your academic advisor at one of the less busy times of the semester. Make the longest appointment possible so that the two of you will have a chance to go beyond the basics of "where are you from?" and "how are your classes going?" If you already have a resumé, bring it along. The two goals of this meeting are for you to become comfortable talking with your advisor, and for him or her to start getting a sense of you as an individual.

If you have an assigned advisor, stay in touch with him or her even if everything is going fine. If you aren't assigned to anyone, shop around for a well-regarded advisor. Schedule an appointment with someone other students recommend; go in with some questions and see if you agree with their assessment. If so, schedule future advising appointments well in advance so your preferred advisor is more likely to be available.

Look for an advisor who:

- Asks you tough questions that make you think.
- Listens carefully.
- Is knowledgeable about the institution, its resources and academic curricula.
- Understands the many ways people learn.

If you find an advisor with these qualities, you have found a treasure—stick to him or her like glue!

YOU HAVE TO SURROUND yourself with other motivated people. I was really lucky; I found a responsible bunch of people to live with my freshman year. We all fed off each other and kept each other in line. We constantly reminded each other not to stay out all night drinking, otherwise we'd end up wasting the next day. It's really easy to fall into the wrong crowd.

> —TIM
> SANTA CRUZ, CALIFORNIA
> SONOMA STATE UNIVERSITY

* * * * * * * * *

I HAD A FRIEND IN THE SAME MAJOR. To help us maintain an A average, we would constantly bet who would get the highest score on our math or engineering tests. We wouldn't bet for money or anything like that; just because we both had a lot of pride and thought we were the smartest.

> —EVENS ALEXIS
> CALUMET CITY, ILLINOIS
> CHICAGO STATE UNIVERSITY

* * * * * * * * *

I'M AN ENGINEERING STUDENT. But sometimes I need a break, so I ask a professor in a completely different field—like psychology or philosophy—if I can sit in on his class. There are so many opportunities to learn about so many things in college and you don't have to sign up for a class or even officially audit it to take advantage of that.

> —THEA
> ST. LOUIS, MISSOURI
> WASHINGTON UNIVERSITY GPA: 3.68

I made the Dean's List, and there is nothing better than feeling like you really accomplished what you set out to do in college.

—A.L.
HILLSBOROUGH, CALIFORNIA
UNIVERSITY OF CALIFORNIA, DAVIS GPA: 3.65

INFORMATION LITERACY: WHY DO YOU NEED IT?

Imagine you are looking at a chart or table on an exam such as the SAT. You could probably understand the chart or table and answer some questions about the information it presents. Information literacy requires you to go even further. Can you evaluate the source of the chart or table to determine whether it is reliable? Can you use the information to answer your own questions about the subject? Can you determine whether you need more information, and figure out how to go about getting it?

An educated person needs to be able to use information in a sophisticated way. Many educators believe that information literacy is one of the most important skills for college students to acquire. And you don't just need information literacy during your college years—you need it all your life. Think of all the information you are bombarded with every day. Think about the information that reaches you through your e-mail account alone. How many e-mails do you receive from total strangers each week inviting you to take advantage of a hot stock tip? It's information literacy that saves you from that kind of scam. And how many pop-up windows inform you that you have just won a free laptop computer while you were surfing the Internet? You get the picture!

THE PERSONAL SATISFACTION of getting a high GPA is one way I stayed motivated as an undergraduate student. However, my desire to get better grades than my boyfriend might have had an even stronger influence. Although we went to different schools and had different majors, we started college at the same time. We kept up a healthy competition with each other; unfortunately I only beat his GPA once.

—PATTY
WHEATFIELD, NEW YORK
NIAGARA UNIVERSITY

* * * * * * * *

I TOOK A YEAR OFF between my sophomore and junior years: I'd burned myself out and wanted to figure out what I was going to do. During my year off, I did an integrated study program of philosophy, world history, and some theology. In my opinion, college is not going to show you who you are: it is going to show you who you could be.

—JONATHAN GARDNER
YREKA, CALIFORNIA
CALIFORNIA INSTITUTE OF TECHNOLOGY

* * * * * * * *

STAYING MOTIVATED IS ABOUT FINDING the right balance. If I can enjoy college a little bit more and end up with a 3.5 GPA instead of a 3.7, I don't stress out about it.

—NAOMI GOLDIN
HAWTHORNE, NEW YORK
CORNELL UNIVERSITY GPA: 3.59

NOT JUST WHERE THEY KEEP THE BOOKS

Why do I need an orientation to a library?

The libraries of modern colleges and universities serve many different functions. Yes, there are books, and quiet places to study. There are also usually extensive electronic resources, and a variety of special services. Many libraries offer tours and electronic tutorials to help students get acquainted with everything. If your professor asked you to find five peer-reviewed articles about research in, say, disability studies, would you know how to search for them? Your library may also be part of a consortium, allowing you to request texts located at other schools.

Take the tour, do the tutorial, and you will thank yourself throughout the next four years.

DON'T FEAR THE TUTORING CENTER

Some of the students you will bump into in the tutoring center are honors students, and I'm not just talking about the ones doing the tutoring. Support services are there to help everyone do their best, not just to bail out people who are failing. This should inspire you to go for two reasons. First, you don't have to worry that walking through the doors will brand you as stupid or incapable. Second, you don't have to wait for an F on a paper or a D on an exam to go for tutoring. You can go because you want to turn that A- into an A. Or you can go because this semester is fine, but you know you'll be taking a few really hard courses next semester and you want to strengthen your study skills. In fact, it's never too early or too late to stop by and see what the tutoring center can offer you.

Do It!
Expectations and Imperatives in College

Regret is a terrible feeling. It can be painful to realize that you could have done or experienced something important but chose not to, especially when the opportunity is unlikely to ever come around again. In this chapter, students will advise you on all kinds of experiences you should make sure to have in college. I agree with just about all of them. Rather than focus on any of those recommendations here, I want to talk about one major obstacle I see a lot of students creating for themselves which prevents them from experiencing all that college has to offer: Working too many hours for pay.

I don't mean waiting tables or working in the registrar's office in order to earn enough to buy your books and your train ticket to go home for winter break. I'm not talking about those of you who absolutely have to work to provide food and shelter for yourself or your family. I'm referring to students who take time away from school because they feel they can't do without a car, expensive clothes, the latest cell phone: in short, luxuries.

It's tough, because our culture tells us we need to be wealthy and, most of all, look wealthy. We are embarrassed to say to our friends, "I can't join you for dinner at that restaurant—I can't afford it." But don't spend so much time working for money for luxuries that you miss out on college experiences that are even more precious. A year or two from now, those designer jeans will be out of style, but the memories and benefits of special college experiences will be part of you forever. Trust me on this one; you won't regret it.

GET THE BEST GRADES POSSIBLE. My grades were average. C. Average. And when I graduated, not one Grade-A accounting firm wanted me because my GPA wasn't a 3.5 or higher, even though I knew how to do the job, and had internships. So after ten years of working, you would think that my experience in accounting would be enough, but it's not. After just applying for a new job, I still had to get a copy of my transcripts. So be aware that your grades will follow you years after college.

—YVETTE DAVIS
CHICAGO, ILLINOIS
UNIVERSITY OF ILLINOIS AT CHICAGO GPA: 2.8

MY FIRST SEMESTER AT COLLEGE, I was living in the university village. One of the RA's decided to set up a huge slip-n-slide across the lawn of the apartment complex. The slip-n-slide was approximately 50 feet long, they used water, dish soap, beer, and whatever else was available to make it slippery. People were riding pool floats, boogie boards, shopping carts, skateboards and whatever else they could find down this slip-n-slide. It was hilarious, it seems like everyone who lived in the complex was taking part in the festivities, which made it extra fun. One big, happy, college party.

—J.B.
RIVERSIDE, CALIFORNIA
CALIFORNIA STATE UNIVERSITY, SAN BERNARDINO

A BIG PART OF BEING A GOOD STUDENT, especially at a big school, is you really have to make school smaller for yourself. You can do this by going to your professor's office hours, by engaging with other students who do well in your courses and really just trying to connect as much as possible with other people.

—DANNY J. HERRERA
LYNWOOD, CALIFORNIA
UNIVERSITY OF CALIFORNIA, BERKELEY

• • • • • • • • •

MY SOPHOMORE YEAR I WORKED for the Rutgers Alumni Association. I was in charge of PR and archival projects. I helped plan Reunion Weekend. This was in my major field. I had to schedule it around classes. It's on my resumé: I think employers look for that. I also learned something I couldn't have learned in class. I got hands-on experience.

—ELIZABETH ALARIO
WARREN, NEW JERSEY
RUTGERS UNIVERSITY

• • • • • • • • •

ONE THING I LEARNED was the importance of saving money, and having some kind of savings plan. I've had a job since my sophomore year, but only this year, as a senior, do I realize I need savings as well as a checking account, because money just disappears. At the end of the semester, I was always wondering where all the money that I worked so hard to earn had gone.

—JOHN KEELEY
MORRISTOWN, NEW JERSEY
HARVARD UNIVERSITY

UNDERSTAND THAT IT IS NO LESS than a gift to be in college. Make a commitment; devote yourself to expanding your mind, doing the work, studying for exams, and doing the best you can. After all, it's the last time in your life that you'll be able to devote yourself to nothing but learning. My parents never complained about it, but I knew it was a tremendous financial strain to put me through college. I felt strongly that taking the work seriously and doing the best I possibly could was a way of showing them that I did not take any of my college education for granted.

—JANE
MONTCLAIR, NEW JERSEY
BARNARD COLLEGE

* * * * * * * *

Don't slack academically, but keep in mind that 10 years from now you'll probably remember a great night out with friends more than you will a grade on a midterm.

—BETH STURGEON
CHICAGO, ILLINOIS

FRAN'S FABLES:
THE HAWK'S CLOUDY WEEK

Most academic disciplines fall under the social science, biological science, humanities, and physical science categories. Each of these categories has its own vocabulary and approach to knowledge. It's important to become conversant with all these modes, although each of us probably feels most comfortable with one of the four...

The Hawk liked to know everything that went on around his mountain. He was famous for having the best eyes of any creature around: from atop his favorite rocky crag, he could see every leaf or pine needle on every tree; every flower; every whisker on every little mouse down below; every feather of every bird up above.

One day a layer of cloud drifted in and obscured the Hawk's upward view. He solved this problem by flying above the clouds to check things out.

The next day a thick fog rolled in. Then the winds died down and the fog just sat there. It filled the valley entirely and extended so high above the mountaintop that the Hawk didn't relish the idea of trying to get through it. What would he do now? He couldn't see a thing!

"My vision *is* my sharpest sense," he thought, "but I suppose I could try another." He sniffed hesitantly at the foggy air, and his rudimentary olfactory nerve came to life. Sure enough, he could smell the new green leaves, the flowers, and the sap-filled evergreens.

By the next day, however, the Hawk had developed a cold. The fog remained, and he could neither see nor smell.

"I suppose I could try something else," he mused. He began to listen very intently, and by following the squeaking of rodents in the valley, he acquired a tasty lunch.

The moral of the story: Explore new modes of understanding the world.

DON'T STUDY ABROAD WITH FRIENDS. Go alone. You'll meet people you wouldn't have met otherwise, and you'll be more likely to talk to the natives if you are not attached to someone else. If you go with friends, you'll stay with them.

> —ELEANOR W. HAND
> ATLANTA, GEORGIA
> UNIVERSITY OF GEORGIA

- - - - - - - -

IN HIGH SCHOOL YOU'RE TAUGHT *what* to think, but in college you're taught to think for yourself. As a result, I've learned to be an active participant in class, asking my professors questions and really exploring the topics and issues we discuss. I believe education should be a two-way street, but so many of my fellow students sit back and let people teach them.

> —ROB J. METZLER
> BUFFALO, NEW YORK
> STATE UNIVERSITY OF NEW YORK, BUFFALO

- - - - - - - -

ONE DAY I SORT OF WOKE UP and said, "Wow! I'm going to be graduating from college and I want to make sure that I lived up to the experience and did everything I wanted to do." I felt like I would miss out if I didn't do it. If you don't get involved in extracurricular activities, I almost guarantee you will regret it.

> —ALEX
> ORANGE COUNTY, CALIFORNIA
> UNIVERSITY OF CALIFORNIA, BERKELEY GPA: 3.79

I studied abroad in Sevilla, Spain. I learned a lot; I lived with a family while I was there. And I met other students from all over the country.

—MOIRA
NEW YORK,
NEW YORK
BOSTON
COLLEGE

Do as many internships as possible during college. This is where you learn the actual skills and experience you will need in the real world. A lot of employers today expect college grads to have experience along with their degrees. Make sure you talk to an advisor about the possibility of doing an internship during the summer, or even during the school year. Oftentimes it will count towards credit hours as well, but even if it doesn't, it's well worth the experience.

—Mandy Takacs
Medina, Ohio
Bowling Green State University

• • • • • • • •

Making lists always works for me, especially lists of my goals. I took a media law class and wrote down on a piece of paper that I wanted to get an A. I posted the paper in my dorm room and carried it around with me as a reminder. I ended up getting an A in the class and actually never did better on a presentation than I did in that class. It might sound weird, but sometimes I think that writing things down is half the battle.

—Liz Pope
Auburn, California
Sonoma State University

SO MANY FRESHMAN ARE INTIMIDATED by what they think will be major intellectual discussions in class. But so much of what we discussed were things like, "What do you call the fizzy drink in a can?" I went to school in St. Louis, and people came from all over the country. Some called it soda pop, some called it soft drinks. My roommate, who was from Texas, would ask me "Can you get me a Coke?" I'd come back with one, when what she wanted was Sprite. Her word for all soda was Coke.

—REBECCA
MOORESTOWN, NEW JERSEY

• • • • • • • • •

THIS MIGHT BE UNIQUE to my college, but they really encourage students to go abroad; perhaps overly so. Your junior year, you just go abroad even if there isn't a good reason to. It's important to consider your own motivation before accepting this. My dad always told me, you only have four years in college. Be in college for those four years and go abroad after. But it turned out the program I went on had a studio architecture program that my college didn't offer, so that was my main reason. I'm glad I went. I don't regret it at all.

—MAGGIE
NEW YORK, NEW YORK
BROWN UNIVERSITY

BON VOYAGE

Study abroad is more popular than ever. In the latest count by the Institute of International Education, more than 200,000 students from the United States were studying abroad each academic year. Why not join them?

One of my regrets about college is that I never studied abroad. I loved my college campus so much, and I was involved in so many activities, that I just didn't think it was possible for me to get away for a whole semester. Plus, studying abroad seemed a little scary. Going to a foreign country where I didn't know anyone, starting over on a new campus, maybe not being able to speak the language very well: it was easy to decide that studying abroad was for other people, but not for me. Now I wish that I had been braver, because I work with many students who have studied abroad and had amazing experiences while doing so. Even if you don't have a lot of money, or you don't speak a foreign language, there are still ways that you can have this experience. Stop by your college's study-abroad office and pick up some materials. Go to an information session or schedule an appointment with the study-abroad advisor. You will be surprised at the many resources that exist to help students go abroad.

SOME OF THE THINGS that made the most profound impact on me were internships and study-abroad programs. It allowed me to put my learning in a completely different context. The classroom experience was informed by cultural experience. That got me thinking on a completely different plane.

—JASON BRUNER
CARTERSVILLE, GEORGIA
GARDNER-WEBB UNIVERSITY

· · · · · · · ·

I THINK THE KEY TO GETTING A'S is to love what you are doing, and if you don't love what you are doing, find a way to make it more interesting. Even if you have to resort to childish things—like, maybe you like the pictures in a certain book or maybe you like how neatly the book is put together. Just find something, anything, that will make you want to read the book. I studied English Literature in undergraduate university in Baghdad, which wasn't very fun, so I had to find some way to like what I was reading. For instance, in my poetry classes I had to find a way to like the poems. I would visualize how the poet sat by candlelight and how he would be really happy seeing thousands of students reading his poems. I imagined him looking at me and being ecstatic because I was reading his work. I never studied for the professors; I studied for the people who wrote the material.

—OMAR FEKEIKI
BERKELEY, CALIFORNIA
ALTURATH UNIVERSITY COLLEGE, BAGHDAD

I COME FROM A VERY SMALL TOWN that is 99-percent white. When I went to college, I was a little apprehensive about all the different cultures I encountered. To find out more, I decided to participate in the Black Student Alliance, the Indian Association, the Filipino Association and the Muslim Association, to name a few. It was really scary at first, because sometimes I was the only white girl in the room. But now, I have a great group of friends I never would have met if I hadn't taken that chance. And I have an appreciation for diversity that will be with me throughout my life.

—MOLLIE G. MOHAN
ROGERSVILLE, MISSOURI
ST. LOUIS UNIVERSITY

- - - - - - - - -

I went to college because I thought it was either go to college or get a job. I knew what I wanted to do with my life; I just didn't know how to get there.

—BETH HARVEY
CHICAGO, ILLINOIS
KENTUCKY WESLEYAN COLLEGE

WHY GETTING A'S IN COLLEGE CAN ACTUALLY BE EASIER THAN GETTING C'S

This is a pet theory of mine, and although I have no research to back it up, my personal experience tells me that it is true. When you make the extra effort to become engaged in your course material, participate actively in class, attend your professor's office hours, and make connections between what you are learning and your own life, you build up momentum.

Soon your work becomes interesting; maybe even enjoyable. Papers are easier to write because you actually have something to say. Exams are easier because you have thought through the material, not just memorized facts. Maybe all of this has taken a bit more time than C-level work, but as they say, time flies when you're having fun!

IF YOU GO TO A BIG SCHOOL where most of your classes are huge, try to find some two-credit classes; they won't do much for your GPA, but you'll get access to your professors in an intimate setting. One of the best things I did in college was when I took a small seminar class. If you are a student who really cares and is engaged with the material, the professor will remember you. You will never get that kind of interaction with a professor if you only take lecture classes with six hundred other students.

—ANONYMOUS
CANOGA PARK, CALIFORNIA
 UNIVERSITY OF CALIFORNIA, BERKELEY GPA: 3.67

• • • • • • • • •

ONE THING EVERY COLLEGE STUDENT needs is an open mind. In high school, you're basically with the same people for years who probably think like you do, so you're not exposed to as many points of view. In an academic setting, you get to talk more freely to people about ideas that you might not have the chance to talk about otherwise. If you're open to it, you can learn to appreciate someone else's perspective. That is so valuable when you get out of college and into the working world where you'll be dealing with all kinds of people.

—LISA E. USCHAKOW
LEVITTOWN, NEW YORK
JOHN JAY COLLEGE OF CRIMINAL JUSTICE

STAYING IN TOUCH AND SHARING YOUR SUCCESSES

One of P.T. Barnum's famous business rules is, "Advertise your business. Do not hide your light under a bushel." One thing many smart kids like best about college is that they no longer feel they have to hide how smart they are. They can let their light shine.

This doesn't mean you should go around bragging, but you can and should share your successes with the people on campus who care about you. Tell your academic advisor when you are chosen for that internship in Washington, D.C. If your first-year English professor helped you a lot, stop by and tell him you're doing well in the sophomore seminar. College faculty and staff love to hear that our students are succeeding. It reaffirms the work that we are doing. It also makes us better able to write strong letters of recommendation when you ask us to.

I WENT TO COLLEGE, but I couldn't really imagine any other path to take. The question really wasn't whether to go to college, but where to go to college. I suppose this expectation came from my parents. There isn't much college can't give you! Not only can college give you an education and the necessary means to get a job you enjoy, but it teaches you many things about life, friendship and growing up that can't be experienced elsewhere. Living on campus with many different people may not always seem so enjoyable at the time, but everyone has a story from when they lived in the dorms and made friends that impacted their life. Living with people, makes you so much more grateful when you do have your own space and teaches you the importance of community.

—Katie Wiese
Chesterton, Indiana
Ball State University

• • • • • • • •

BEFORE I GRADUATED, I immersed myself in a lot of cultures. I went on a trip with my campus church to Japan, I became a conversation partner with a student from Thailand, and I got lucky to get a Greek roommate. I learned so much about their food, beliefs, family, and dance that I feel as if I've been adopted.

—Karinne Spencer
Chicago, Illinois
Southern Illinois University

IF I COULD RECOMMEND ONE THING to do in college, it is to not get stuck with only one circle of friends. Put yourself in situations that force you to interact with people different than yourself. By the time college was over, I had played broomball, gone backpacking to a black sand beach, road tripped to a music festival, and had a ton of other memorable experiences because I tried hanging out with people that I never would have hung out with when I began college.

—EUGENE
FOSTER CITY, CALIFORNIA
UNIVERSITY OF CALIFORNIA, BERKELEY

· · · · · · · · ·

YOU MUST GO TO THE BASKETBALL and football games while you are in college. Nothing made me feel prouder to be a part of my school than having the students, professors, cheerleaders, the dean, the president, and the mascot coming together as a family, forgetting about exams, papers, and hating each other. One night everybody gets along to cheer our team to victory, even if you know they are not going to the playoffs.

—TRACEY HARRIS
CHICAGO, ILLINOIS
UNIVERSITY OF ILLINOIS

WHAT A'S REPRESENT

Earning A's to Prepare for Postgraduate Study

By earning lots of A's, you will make yourself a more competitive candidate for graduate or professional school, and you will develop the skills necessary to succeed in that type of advanced study.

Earning A's to Prepare for Employment

Earning strong grades, especially in the classes where good grades don't come to you so easily, is a great preparation for the world of work. If you earn A's easily—great. If you earn A's through lots of hard work—even better. Employers want to hire people who know how to work hard and are not daunted by a challenge.

I THOUGHT CLASSES WOULD BE EASY, and the bulk of college would be social and fun. I even thought somehow, I would just get smarter by enrolling. It was nothing like that. It was about taking tests, writing papers, work-study, and wishing for the day the four-year nightmare would end.

—ANONYMOUS
CHICAGO, ILLINOIS
UNIVERSITY OF PENNSYLVANIA GPA: 3.72

YOU MUST BECOME GREEK before you graduate. I thought my fun would just be spent drinking, partying, and hanging with the ladies, and it partly was. But I learned true brotherhood, when my fraternity would give food to the homeless, clean shelters, visit sick patients in the hospital, and not be afraid to get emotional.

—BRIAN STANLEY
CHICAGO, ILLINOIS
ROBERT MORRIS COLLEGE

• • • • • • • •

EVERY COLLEGE STUDENT NEEDS to experience the whole four years. Don't try to cram it into three or even two years, leave early, and think you achieved something. You will miss out on a lot because you took so many classes that you couldn't have any fun.

—TSHINO KANKWENDA
MONTREAL, CANADA
SOUTHERN ILLINOIS UNIVERSITY

• • • • • • • •

COLLEGE ISN'T COLLEGE if you don't travel for winter, spring, and summer breaks. Go to Cancun, Europe—even visit a farm. Travel as much as you can, because when you start working in Corporate America, traveling will be rare, except if it's on business, and that's never fun.

—B.M.
COLUMBIA, SOUTH CAROLINA
UNIVERSITY OF SOUTH CAROLINA

COLLEGE = INDEPENDENCE. I am ready to start making my own decisions about my life, instead of living by my parent's expectations. I love having their support, but I'd love having the ability to support myself as well.

—MAREN REISCH
GENEVA, NEW YORK

• • • • • • • • •

BEFORE I WENT TO COLLEGE one of my high school teachers and mentors told me, "Don't let your classes get in the way of your education." I understood what he meant at the time, but didn't truly appreciate it until much later. One of my advisors always said, "Leave things better than you found them." I still hold this with me to this day and try to apply it to all that I do.

—KATIE WIESE
CHESTERTON, INDIANA
BALL STATE UNIVERSITY

SPECIAL THANKS

Thanks to our intrepid "headhunters" for going out to find so many respondents from around the country with interesting advice to share:

Jamie Allen, Chief Headhunter

Andrea Parker	Helen Bond	Nick Resnik
Andrea Syrtash	Jennifer Doll	Paula Andruss
Daniel Drew	John Nemo	Sally Burns
Daniel Nemet-	Lorraine Calvacca	Stacey Shannon
Nejat	Marie Suszynski	Staci Siegel
Gloria Averbuch	Nancy Larson	Terry Selucky

Thanks, too, to our editorial advisor Anne Kostick. And thanks to our assistant, Miri Greidi, for her yeoman's work at keeping us all organized. The real credit for this book, of course, goes to all the people whose experiences and collective wisdom make up this guide. There are too many of you to thank individually, but you know who you are.

CREDITS

Page 40:   Sarah Grimké; Letters on the Equality of the
Sexes and Other Essays, Edited and with an
Introduction by Elizabeth Ann Bartlett, 1988,
Yale University Press, New Haven and London.

Page 167: http://www.med.umich.edu/opm/news-
page/2005/residentsleep.htm

Page 176: Patricia Peterson, Director of Career Services
at the University of the Sciences in Philadelphia

Page 261: http://idcs0100.lib.iup.edu/WestCivl/life_of_the_stu-
dent.htm

Page 279: http://opendoors.iienetwork.or

Praise for HUNDREDS OF HEADS® *Guides:*

"Hundreds of Heads is an innovative publishing house ... Its entertaining and informative 'How To Survive ...' series takes a different approach to offering advice. Thousands of people around the nation were asked for their firsthand experiences and real-life tips in six of life's arenas. Think 'Chicken Soup' meets 'Zagats,' says a press release, and rightfully so."

—ALLEN O. PIERLEONI
"BETWEEN THE LINES," *THE SACRAMENTO BEE*

"A concept that will be ... a huge seller and a great help to people. I firmly believe that today's readers want sound bytes of information, not tomes. Your series will most definitely be the next 'Chicken Soup.'"

—CYNTHIA BRIAN
TV/RADIO PERSONALITY, BEST SELLING AUTHOR: *CHICKEN SOUP FOR THE GARDENER'S SOUL; BE THE STAR YOU ARE!; THE BUSINESS OF SHOW BUSINESS*

"Move over, 'Dummies'... Can that 'Chicken Soup'! Hundreds of Heads are on the march to your local bookstore!"

—ELIZABETH HOPKINS
KFNX (PHOENIX) RADIO HOST, *THINKING OUTSIDE THE BOX*

"The series ... could be described as 'Chicken Soup for the Soul' meets 'Worst Case Scenario.'"

—RACHEL TOBIN RAMOS
ATLANTA BUSINESS CHRONICLE

Other titles in the HUNDREDS OF HEADS® series:

HOW TO SURVIVE YOUR FRESHMAN YEAR

"This book proves that all of us are smarter than one of us."
> —JOHN KATZMAN
> FOUNDER AND CEO, PRINCETON REVIEW

"Voted in the Top 40 Young Adults Nonfiction books."
> —PENNSYLVANIA SCHOOL LIBRARIANS ASSOCIATION

"This cool new book ... helps new college students get a head start on having a great time and making the most of this new and exciting experience."
> —COLLEGE OUTLOOK

HOW TO SURVIVE YOUR FIRST JOB (or Any Job)

Hundreds of gainfully employed, recently out of college, young people offer the best tips, stories, and advice on how to survive your job. Learn the best strategies for landing a first job, launching a career, and succeeding (or just hanging in there) at work. Get great tips on dealing with difficult bosses, odd coworkers, suboptimal environments and tasks, and climbing (or slipping down) the corporate ladder.

HOW TO SURVIVE THE REAL WORLD

"Stories, tips, and advice from hundreds of college grads who found out what it takes to survive in the real world."

—WENDY ZANG
KNIGHT RIDDER/TRIBUNE NEWS SERVICE

"Perfect gift for the newly minted college graduates on your list."

—FRAN HAWK
THE POST AND COURIER (CHARLESTON, SC)

BE THE CHANGE!

"This is a book that could change your life. Read the stories of people who reached out to help somebody else and discovered they were their own ultimate beneficiary. It's almost magic and it could happen to everyone. Go!"

—JIM LEHRER
EXECUTIVE EDITOR AND ANCHOR, NEWSHOUR WITH JIM LEHRER

"An inspiring look at the profound power of the individual to make a positive difference in the lives of others. *Be the Change!* Is more than an eloquent tribute to volunteer service—it increases awareness of our shared humanity."

—ROXANNE SPILLETT
PRESIDENT, BOYS & GIRLS CLUBS OF AMERICA

"Civic involvement is an enriching joy, as the people in this book make clear. It's also what makes America so great. This is a wonderful and inspiring book."

—WALTER ISAACSON
CEO, ASPEN INSTITUTE

ABOUT THE EDITOR

FRANCES NORTHCUTT is an academic advisor in the William E. Macaulay Honors College of the City University of New York at Hunter College. Her advising career began when she became a peer advisor at Wesleyan University, where she earned her BA in English. She went on to advise students at the University of California, Berkeley; and the University of the Sciences in Philadelphia, where she also taught classes on college skills and professional development. Frances is active in the National Academic Advising Association: she has presented at regional conferences, and was selected as the Outstanding Advisor (Primary Role) for the Mid-Atlantic region in 2006. She is currently working on a master's degree in Higher Education Administration at Temple University.

VISIT WWW.HUNDREDSOFHEADS.COM

Do you have something interesting to say about marriage, your in-laws, dieting, holding a job, or one of life's other challenges?

- Help humanity—share your story!
- Get published in our next book!
- Find out about the upcoming titles in the HUNDREDS OF HEADS® survival guide series!
- Read up-to-the-minute advice on many of life's challenges!
- Sign up to become an interviewer for one of the next HUNDREDS OF HEADS® survival guides!